# STYLE & CLASS

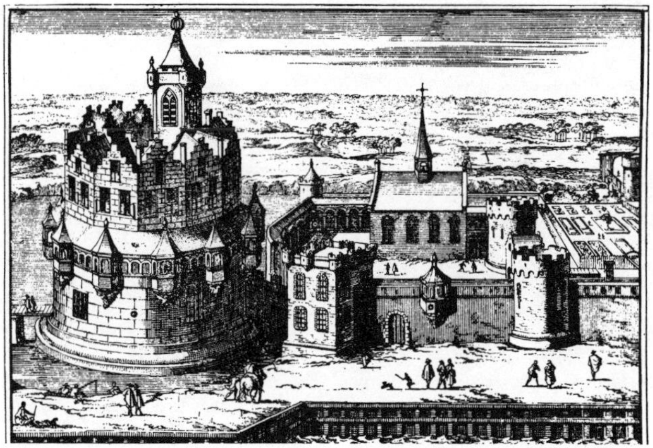

*Also by Sietze Buning:*

**Purpaleanie and other Permutations**
Middleburg Press, 1978

# STYLE AND CLASS

## SIETZE BUNING

Middleburg Press

1982

Orange City, Iowa

**STYLE AND CLASS**

Although this book includes names of some persons, places, and events whose existence is a matter of fact, their presentation here is a matter of fiction. Verification must be by the imagination and not by the official record.



Printed and bound in the United States of America.

10 9 8 7 6 5 4 3 2 1

Editorial adviser was James Vanden Bosch.

Book and cover design are by Carl Vandermeulen.

The designs on the cover are motifs from Dutch cross-stitch samplers of the seventeenth, eighteenth, and nineteenth centuries. The designs were originally created by women and girls who took time from busy and often difficult lives to add style, stitch by stitch, to homes, churches, and clothing. Needlework by Jan Vandermeulen.

*Library of Congress Cataloging in Publication Data*

*Buning, Sietze, 1930-*
*Style and class.*

*I. Title.*
*PS 3573.I358S78 1982 811'.54 82-14541*
*ISBN 0-931940-06-0*

The Middleburg Press
Box 166, 403 Third St. N.W.
Orange City, Iowa 51041

*voor Hendrik Zijlstra, de prins,*

*die tijdelijk ver weg zijn adventuuren drijft*

> *"Wij steken't hoofd omhoog, en zullen d'eerkroon dragen"*
> (uit Psalm 89, de oude berijming door J. Eusebius Voet, 1773)

*en voor zijn prinsesse, Mildred, die hem moedig navolgt*

> *"Hart, onrustig, vol van zorgen,*
> *vleugellam geslagen ziel,*
> *hoop op God en wees geborgen.*
> *Hij verheft wie nederviel."*
> (uit Psalm 42, de nieuwe berijming door W. Barnard, 1968)

# CONTENTS

## THE TERMS



## LETTING MIDDLEBURG GO

## LETTING THE TERMS GO



## A TALE OF TWO TOWNS

## *A Translation*

(*Lord's Day XII from* The Heidelberg Catechism, *1563*)

31 Q. Why is he called *Christ*
meaning "anointed"?

A. Because he has been ordained by God the Father
and has been anointed with the Holy Spirit
to be
our chief prophet and teacher
who perfectly reveals to us
the secret counsel and will of God for our deliverance;
our only high priest
who has set us free by the one sacrifice of his body
and who continually pleads our cause with the Father;
and our eternal king
who governs us by his Word and Spirit,
and who guards and safeguards the freedom
he has won for us.

32 Q. But why are you called a Christian?

A. Because by faith I am a member of Christ
and so I share in his anointing.
I am anointed
to confess his name,

to present myself to him as a living sacrifice of thanks,

to strive with a free conscience against sin and the devil
in this life,
and afterward to reign with him
over all creation
for all eternity.

*Translated by the Heidelberg Catechism Translation Committee of the Christian Reformed Church, 1975*

*Clarence Boersma*
*Sietze Buning*
*Fred H. Klooster, chairman*
*Edward J. Masselink*
*Richard F. Wevers, secretary*
*Stanley Wiersma*
*Sierd Woudstra*

# Style & Class

# THE TERMS

WILLEM DE EERSTE, PRINS VAN ORANJE

# *Dominie, in 1943, Struggles with Lord's Day XII, from 1563*



Beloved congregation—

Why do you call your Savior *Christ*, "anointed"?
I'll live and die by words of Christ the Prophet.
Himself the sacrifice, he is my Priest.
Of microbes, galaxies, my middling life—he's King.
(One mediator whose three tasks come disjointed?
Three school abstractions all together pieced?)

Though sacrificed, his kingliness increases.
He'll come with fire, this royal judge appointed—
yet never was so meek a priest anointed.
Distinguishing this trinity takes a prophet,
to tell how the Victim-Victor, the Priestly King,
sets off the Victor-Victim, the Royal Priest.

And why are you called Christian? I'm a priest
and only in self-sacrifice find peace.
My folks are common folks, yet I'm a king.
Nobody plot against the Lord's anointed!
Though my words chatter his Word, I'm a prophet.
To teach, and sacrifice, and rule is my appointment.

This trinity is mine in Christ's anointing.
Not wordless, lacking majesty, playing at priest.
Not selfish, lacking majesty, playing at prophet.
Our world lacks majesty, its power in pieces.
A president or captain's not anointed,
but Christians are anointed queen or king.

How can we learn to be a queen or king?
Today's officials, elected and appointed,
have style—but few the class of one anointed.
Not President and Priest, but King and Priest.
The three-in-one anointings seem to cease.
Unless we're royalty, we're not priests and prophets.

In teachers and in preachers we have prophets,
but where the pattern for a queen or king?
As parliamentary monarch's majesty decreases,
more power rests with officialdom appointed. 14
Each act of selfless love defines a priest,
but where some proper royalty anointed?
A prophet-teacher, a sacrificing priest,
and mighty king make up one great anointing.
Lose one, like king, three pieces lie disjointed.

Amen.

*Dominie, in 1943,*
*Struggles with Lord's Day XII,*
*from 1563*

# *Sietze Sees Dominie about a Sermon*

Ja, Dominie,
on Sunday you said officialdom, elected and appointed,
has style,
but that anointed kings and queens
have class.
To me they sound the same.

Well, Sietze,
style needs to be noticed to get votes.
Class is the same, noticed or unnoticed.

Style you imitate from friends or radio
(television wasn't around yet)
but class you're born with or adopted into.

You like my tie, you buy one like it
(he would have said T-shirt today),
you fix up your kitchen like *Kitchen Clatter Magazine*
(he would have said *House Beautiful* today),
you sing "Tangerine" this week
(he would have said "My Sharona" today—
always a little out of it)—
that's style.
And style is good.
You need some of it.
But style is not required by the Catechism
(he would have said "laid on us" today).

You learn to do what's right
like it or not
or learn to like it.
When in the right
you're royally indifferent
to being different.
You like what is best
or try to like what's best
whether the best is old or new—
that's class.

16

*Sietze Sees Dominie*
*about a Sermon*

Style reads its history in the newspaper,
and history starts with the Titanic
(he would have said Watergate today).
Class is curious about Alexander and Julius Caesar,
about King Alfred and Eleanor of Aquitaine,
about King Floris and his five dogs,
about the myths surrounding King Arthur and Tintagel.
Class remembers what kings and queens are like.

Ja, Dominie,
but I don't feel like a king
and you don't look much like one either.
Tell me one time when you were a king.

(The pause was so long that Sietze thought
Dominie had started an argument inside
against Arminians on the one side
or Herman Hoeksema on the other.)

Ja, Sietze,
one time I know I was a king.
Twenty-two of us were in the courthouse
being naturalized:
one Dane, two Norwegians, a dozen Poles,
and seven of us Dutch.
Time came for each of us to renounce our countries.
I could not bring myself to renounce Queen Wilhelmina.
I got behind the Dane who said,
"I hereby renounce allegiance to King Frederick of Denmark."
I also renounced allegiance to King Frederick of Denmark.
Nobody noticed.
I vote here, but I never renounced the House of Orange.
That day, maybe I had some class.
That day, I was a little like a king.

# *Wilhelmina*



Queen Wilhelmina
was entertaining the Frisian Cattle Breeders' Association
at dinner.

The Frisian farmers
didn't know what to make of their finger bowls.
They drank them down.

The stylish courtiers from the Hague
nudged each other, and pointed, and laughed
at such lack of style.

Until the queen herself
without a smile
raised her finger bowl and drained it
obliging all the courtiers to follow suit
without a smile.

The courtiers had style
but Queen Wilhelmina had class.

# *Juliana*

Queen Juliana came to visit a campus—
which shall go unnamed.
The professors in caps and gowns lined the sidewalks,
an honor guard,
while the College President escorted the Queen and Prince Bernhard
into the chapel for a convocation.

An elderly professor,
too deaf to know how loud he talked,
broke the solemn stillness
by announcing to nobody in particular:
*"Wat heeft zij tog dikke benen!"*
("What fat legs she's got!")
Everybody heard him.
Queen Juliana too.

She stopped in front of him,
smiled,
and said with an arch playfulness:
*"Mijnheer, daar moet het hele Oranjehuis op rusten."*
("Sir, these legs need to hold up the whole House of Orange.")
Everyone in earshot cheered.

No question about it,
the old professor lacked style
but nobody minded
because Queen Juliana had such class.

# *Holy Water*
*(for Tom and Elaine)*

It was style in Middleburg church for Albert van Dongen,
the janitor, to sit alone in the front pew.
He had to pump the organ.

It is style in all Reformed churches
for the janitor to put a glass of water
inside the pulpit in case the dominie gets thirsty.

One Sunday just as Dominie was starting his second point
his mouth turned dry and he reached for a glass of water
that was not there.
Albert had actually forgotten.
Having no rock to strike,
Dominie turned to Albert and rasped out:
"Mr. van Dongen, I would like some water."
Albert was, in fact, sleeping as soundly as a rock.
It was his style after Dominie's first point.
An awkward pause.
"Mr. van Dongen."
Another awkward pause.

Dad,
clerk of the consistory
and seated at the end of the consistory pew,
had a choice: get the water and let Albert sleep,
or do what he did—
walk up to Albert,
shake him awake,
and order water for Dominie.
Nobody should be asleep,
so it was not a difficult decision.

Albert all but ran out:
"Water?
Water, ja. Water."
But alone in the consistory room
the purpose for the water was unclear.

And so Albert appeared with water all right,
but it was in the baptismal basin.

Fortunately we Reformed aren't stuck on holy vessels
or Dominie would have had to send him back for a glass.
As it was, Dominie turned his back to the congregation,
leaned forward, and sucked out of the middle of the basin
like a horse.
The brim would have been too wide.
Water would have streamed all over his clothes.
Baptism is just as effective out of a casserole, isn't it?
So why not drink out of a baptismal basin?
Any Reformed dominie would have done the same,
so that was only style,
as were Albert's sleeping, Albert's mistake,
and Dad's waking him up.

Whose then was the class?
The congregation's.

That congregation witnessed Albert caught asleep,
and Dad's waking him;
the baptismal basin in Albert's hand,
and Dominie's drinking from it—
legs spread wide and leaning forward
like a giraffe.
Yet the first sound
in addition to the clock's suddenly deafening tick
was Dominie's resuming his sermon at point two.

Of course,
after the benediction
we young folks burst out of the church doors
doubled over and stamping our feet.

At dinner
when Dad thought of it
midway through a spoonful of pea soup,
he sprayed great green blotches
all over Mother's white tablecloth.

Even today,
all I need to do to make my brother yelp with laughter
is to take Dominie's pose, sucking up that water.

If anyone had tittered when it happened
the whole congregation would have been beside themselves.

But nobody did.

Everybody was a king or queen.

At state occasions, royalty is not amused.

# *Bells*

It was the style in my church for Dominie,
as catechism teacher, to treat the pupils
after the last lesson in spring.
It was useful for making up.
The custom said,
"Next year hostilities will set in again,
but now we're friends."

One May,
when we had devoured Dominie's treat,
he asked whether I had ever seen the bell.
I hadn't, so he showed me.
Up to the balcony,
through a trapdoor,
up a winding stair,
up a ladder, and there was the bell,
bigger than I had expected even.

Why me?
I had been no better than the others
and deserved no special prize.
I had been no worse than the others
so the cookies should have done for making up.
And as for a bribe,
he might have known it wouldn't stick over the summer.

He did it because all love is election.
Somebody from the next generation
would need to be interested in bells
or bells would go the way of tails.

As bells have.
I moved away and attend a church without a bell.
Bells are out of style.

But ever since that day
it has been my style
to choose guided tours of belfries—
in Chichester, Groningen, and Geneva—
but no guided tour of a belfry ever has as much class.

I was called.

# *Country Wedding*
*(for Dave and Pat)*

---



Amused and embarrassed by home
after my first year away at college,
I now knew that the processional music from *Lohengrin*,
the march from Mendelssohn's *Midsummer Night's Dream*,
and assorted trumpet voluntaries by Purcell
were the only items on a closed list of wedding music
approved by People Who Know.
I had deliberately forgotten after only a year, city-style,
how clutched I had been when Pete and Margaret
took their places in the parlor
under an arch trimmed in yellow and orange,
the bride's chosen colors,
while a baritone cousin of Pete's sang to his wife's guitar
"You won't have to cross Jordan alone."

When pressed I now argued that "You won't have to cross Jordan alone"
is a song about death, and, therefore, had been wrong for the wedding,
deliberately forgetting after only a year, city-style,
that the prospect of having somebody around when you die
is a fringe benefit of marriage not to be minimized.

I also argued that "You won't have to cross Jordan alone"
means that Jesus, not your marriage partner,
will be with you when you die,
deliberately forgetting after only a year, city-style,
that husbands and wives
can do the work of Jesus for each other.

And I argued that the emphasis in "You won't have to cross Jordan alone"
is on the word *alone*. Bringing up *alone* at all at the wedding
had been wrong, I insisted,
deliberately forgetting after only a year, city-style,
that even married, we are, each of us,
very much alone.

Besides, I added as a clincher, "You won't have to cross Jordan alone"
is insufferably bland music,
and I showed off what I now knew
about parallel thirds and sixths
and about the use of dominant sevenths and diminished sevenths
in the nineteenth century, which I had learned to loathe,
deliberately forgetting after only a year, city-style,
that the harmony of "Jordan" is no more insufferably bland
than the city's closed and predictable list of wedding music,
be its harmony ever so interesting.



Even after my college critique, "You won't have to cross Jordan alone"
would still be Pete's choice, he insisted,
though Margaret regretted that Sietze didn't go to college a year before
so he could have helped plan it proper-like.
"Margaret, you could have had style given the opportunity," I said,
deliberately forgetting after only a year, city-style,
how transparent city condescension is.

How great to be free from "You won't have to cross Jordan alone"
and from all songs like it, I thought but did not say.
How great to be free! —
deliberately forgetting after only a year, city-style,
that all freedoms are relative,
that any couple in Middleburg is free to choose Purcell
provided somebody in the church learns to play it.

It must have been in the city itself
I picked up the notion that I had come to the city to be free,
deliberately forgetting after only a year, city-style,
how quaint the freedom of the city had struck me at first.
Not only didn't it bother me any more
that "You won't have to cross Jordan alone"
was not likely to appear during the current season
on the city's immutable list of wedding music
approved by People Who Know.
I was downright happy to be free—
city-style—
but I had lost whatever class I had a claim to.

# *Kyrie*



My first Christmas home from college
Dad wondered what I learned
in those expensive piano lessons.

"Style, Dad, style."

"Let's hear some of that style."

"Well, this is the baroque style, Dad."

I bypassed *The Well-Tempered Clavichord* and *French Suites*
and eased Dad into the baroque with Myra Hess's transcription
of "Jesu, Joy of Man's Desiring."

Afterwards silence.

"How do you like the baroque style, Dad?"

"Oh, I don't know.
As far as I can judge
the baroque style is pretty much
whippity whuppity whuppity
whuppity whippity whippity."

So I tried the classical-turning-romantic style
of Beethoven's "Pathetique."

Dad liked it no better.
It was all "BOOM
b-boom b-boom boom."

So I tried impressionism,
Debussy's "Sunken Cathedral."

It was worst of all.
"Azzzzzzzzzzzzzz
mmmmmmmmmmmmm
zzzzzzzzzzzzzzzz."

I knew what Dad wanted
and I gave it:
Psalm 51 from *The Genevan Psalter.*

He found my playing of it lovely,
worth every penny of those expensive lessons
though I could play it before I ever left home.

The next week the new semester in music theory
began with a lecture by a Jewish musicologist
from the state university.
His subject: *The Genevan Psalter.*

"You American Calvinists have done pretty well in preserving
the major and minor melodies of *The Genevan Psalter.*
Psalms 42, 68, and 73 are all in your *Psalter Hymnal.*
But the finest Genevan melodies are not in major or minor,
but in the dorian, phrygian, and lydian modes.
You have let all those interesting melodies fade
just at a time when contemporary composers are turning toward
the medieval modes again. Just wait,
some composer is going to snap up all those Genevan melodies
just when you have let them go. For instance,
is there anybody here in music theory at Calvin College
who knows Psalm 51, the Calvinist *kyrie* in the phrygian mode?"

My hand was the only one to go up.

"You mean you can sing it?"

I did,
right from the solemn opening

to the heavy phrygian close

The Jewish musicologist led the applause afterwards 28
and insisted that hearing the Genevan 51
as preserved in a folk tradition *Kyrie*
had been worth his whole trip to Grand Rapids.

And I thought it hardly mattered
that Dad knew so little about musical style
seeing he had such class.

# *Tillie*

*(for Marie Post)*



Tillie, our hired girl, was jittery.
When she started laughing, she always ended up crying.
"It would help if she had Jesus in her heart," Mother said.
Dad said, "Now don't go off half-cocked inviting her to church.
We hired her Mondays through Fridays
and leave well enough alone."
Tillie was a fallen-away Lutheran.
Her brother-in-law and sister got her every Friday night
and brought her back—tired—on Monday morning.
They were from Hawarden, twenty miles away,
at the edge of the Dutch community.

Mother let the matter rest for now.
Dominie was taking his time with the sin-and-misery
part of the catechism—sermons not likely to take.
When Dominie's next sermon was going to be
"What is true faith?"
Mother invited Tillie to stay for the weekend.

All Saturday afternoon Mother rehearsed her
on when to stand, when to sit with eyes open,
when to sit with eyes closed, and how to pass the plate
without obviously looking at how much your neighbor put in.

Mother forgot to brief Tillie on Mrs. Zoetekoek,
and on Sunday the Zoetekoeks sat directly ahead of us.
Just as Dominie warmed up to his second point—
that faith is not only a sure knowledge but a blessed assurance too—
Mrs. Zoetekoek cried out in what sounded like ecstasy
and stiffened up.
It was a seizure we were all used to.
Her sons and her husband carried her out into the consistory room.
We had scarcely begun to be blessedly assured
when we heard an ecstatic cry from Tillie.
She had stiffened up just like Mrs. Zoetekoek.
Dad, Mother, and I weren't nearly as practiced as the Zoetekoeks
at carrying out ecstatics.
I carried her shoulders high enough,
but Dad couldn't hoist her middle high enough,
and Mother followed,
vainly trying to pick up Tillie's dragging feet.
Mother was too gussied up to bend down that far.

At home, Tillie rested on the couch in the living room.
Mother in the kitchen over coffee:
"She was struck down like Saul on the way to Damascus
just when Dominie started in about assurance."

"Nonsense," Dad said.
"She got excited from seeing Mrs. Zoetekoek's fit
and she had one of her own."

"Sure, sure," said Mother,
"explain it away.
And explain too why Mrs. Zoetekoek only gets her spells in church."

"Oh, and now," said Dad,
"Mrs. Zoetekoek's fits are all Damascus-road experiences too.
St. Paul didn't need but one to get turned around."

"I suppose," Mother said,
"you consider St. Paul's Damascus-road experience
an epileptic fit, you modernist."

"Poor Tillie," Dad said.
"She probably thought we Reformed all do like Mrs. Zoetekoek
when we get the Spirit."

"Who are you to say Tillie was faking?"
Mother asked,

and of their vain contest appeared no end—
not ever.

Into old age
Mother claimed Tillie as a star in her crown,
flying in the face of all Dad's evidence.
That took class.



Flying in the face of all Mother's evidence,
Tillie never came to church with us again.
Soon after, she went to business college in Omaha.
Two years later she married an evangelist.

Flying in the face of this outcome,
Dad still would not grant Tillie a Damascus-road experience.
His reason, I'm afraid, was very much in the Christian Reformed style:

"She didn't know enough doctrine to deserve one."

# LETTING MIDDLEBURG GO

*Learned in Orange City*

Love is to hang on
and
love is to let go.
To do the one
without at the same time
doing the other
is not love.

## *Hull Humanity*

"Hey, here's your sandwich," I called across the lunchroom
to Caldwell, the kid we picked on.
He was fat and unathletic,
and we kept him in his place.

Right in style,
I threw the sandwich I had swiped from him. He reached,
missed,
and the waxed paper burst apart
against the lunchroom window.
A smear of mayonnaise streaked the glass,
a flap of bologna hung over the back of a desk,
a lettuce leaf and a tomato slice lay on the floor.
I smiled triumphantly,
the boys' lunchroom laughed adoringly,
and then we heard Mr. Leonard's voice.
He had stepped in without our noticing.

"Caldwell,
here is my sandwich.
Enjoy it.
Sietze,
may I see you out in the hall?"

"OH oh."
"Naughty Sietze."
"Now you'll catch it."
I was afraid.

In the hall
Mr. Leonard said quietly,
"People throw food only at animals."

"Yes, Mr. Leonard," I said.
He did not need to tell me to go for
mop, cloth, and soapy water.

From then on
Caldwell was different for me
and I was decent to him.

Once or twice later
I have felt as alienated as Caldwell must have then.
Depressed,
I can always find comfort
in how efficiently a waitress pours my coffee,
in how a check-out girl smiles as she makes change,
and in how you, dear, ladle me a bowl of cheese soup
        and wipe the inside of the rim
        so that the line of yellow-green soup
        will be sharp against the brown pottery,
and I remember that people throw food only to animals,
and I tell myself,
"Sietze, you're not such a dog as you think you are."

# *The Edgerton Fern*



Grandma Groen inherited a fern from her mother
and in turn passed on baby ferns to her daughters,
daughters-in-law, sisters, granddaughters, nieces, and friends.
Anyone who knew her had part of Grandma's fern.

Of all the younger ferns,
none was so thriving as Grandma's own.
She watered it twice a week
and transplanted it every other spring,
but always planted it back in the old pot,
a big one of green-glazed pottery,
the same pot that had been her mother's.

Time came for Grandma Groen to move to an old folk's home.
The fern was the last object to leave the house.
She and two daughters carried it—
carefully out of the front door,
carefully down the front steps,
carefully toward the waiting station wagon.

Midway between house and station wagon
the bottom of the pot dropped out
and the sides collapsed.
In the middle of the sidewalk lay shards of green-glazed pottery
and a whole bushel of dirt and fern.

Grandma Groen's only comment had class:
"God knows I've always been too proud of it."

# *Henry Beets in Rudyard*

*(for Mother Grace)*

---



Rudyard,
in Michigan's Upper Peninsula,
thinks that preachers visiting from Grand Rapids have style.
They drive up in air-conditioned Electras,
wear golfing clothes en route,
maroon slacks and white jackets for Saturday dinner,
and black suits with maroon ties on Sunday.
Coming and going,
they stop for coffee in view of the Mackinac Bridge.
They take pictures with Leicas.
They have style.

In the old days before the bridge,
Henry Beets wore one outfit
for train, ferry, car, table, and pulpit:
a swallowtail coat with striped trousers,
with wing collar and black bow tie.

One Monday morning when roads were bad,
his host made it to the dock with his Model A
after the captain's orders to loosen moorings.
The captain was about to order the gangplank hoisted
when he saw Beets getting out of the car.
He called to Beets on his bullhorn:
"Get the lead out, sir, if you want to ride!"
Beets stopped.
His hand went up as in benediction.
What he said was louder even than the captain's bullhorn:
"HOLD YOUR PEACE!"

When it was clear that the ferry would wait,
Beets proceeded,
no faster than before.

As the host reported it,
and as Rudyard remembers it,
and as I heard it,
Beets had no style at all,
but he sure had class.

# *The Saugatuck Pledge*

*(for W. Harry Jellema)*

Bart came home from a midweek meeting late at night.
Mary was nursing the sick Bart Jr.;
she was glad Bart Sr. was home.
None of their three older girls had ever been so hot to her touch.
The only time he stopped his whimpering was when she nursed him,
as she was doing now,
even though within the hour he would be throwing up.
Bart Sr. was home now, and that made it easier.
"What happened at the meeting?" she asked.
Some quiet talk would help the milk to flow.

"Well," said Bart,
"Dominie Krop gave a speech
on changing the American culture around us
and how the school is really the best way to do it.
At the end of the meeting he took pledges of time and money
to support the new school.
Piet Niemoller pledged a hundred dollars
and just like that there must have been ten other pledges.
Some gave as much as Piet, some less."

"How much did you pledge, Bart?"

"I pledged a week of carpentry
next fall when the crops are in."

"Money, I mean."

"I didn't pledge any money.
We haven't been here as long as the Niemollers, you know.
Our livestock and farm machinery isn't even paid off yet.
We need an extra team of horses to pull the new gangplow
we had to borrow for.
Maybe next year we will make a pledge."

Mary thought for a moment.
"But we need a school for our children this year, Bart.
If we don't give God what's his right—
a school to help make his Kingdom come—
couldn't he take what's ours
like our poor sick Barty?"

She could feel the milk stop,
and the baby whimpered.

Bart said,
"That's superstitious, Mary.
We can't buy the baby's health from God."



Mary knew that and was silent.
The baby whimpered harder.

"But," said Bart, "if you think we can manage it,
I could go see Dominie tomorrow
and pledge, say, a hundred like Niemoller.
Whether we keep Barty or lose him,
we still can give the money for the school."

Mary felt the milk return
and Barty sucked again,
hard.

Now, don't call it class right away
that next day Bart pledged his hundred.
There was some social pressure in it,
a frontier notion of not letting the community down,
and, let's face it, it was a shrewd investment.
Anywhere a Christian school is established
at parents' expense,
there are stories like it,
right from the 1890's, when Bart made his pledge,
right through the 1980's.

It is a pattern.
And in the 1940's
young Barty gave up a chairmanship
at a wealthy state university
to teach philosophy in a Christian college
at half the salary.
There was some social pressure in it,
a frontier notion of not letting the community down,
and, let's face it, it was a shrewd investment
seeing his own children were of college age.
They would have gone to the Christian college in any case
and this way they could live at home.

Each sacrifice alone
is no more than the Christian style.
It is the pattern that has the class.

# *The Sea of Forgetfulness: Lake Michigan*

*(for Ed Ericson)*



With style Dominie and I brought *huisbezoek*
to Willem's Holland Home bedside.
I read Psalm 46.
Dominie praised his regular attendance.
I took note that his budget was all paid up:
"More than a tenth of your old age pension, Willem."
Dominie urged him to join a grow group in the Home—
one that would meet right at his bedside.
I praised his weathering Nelly's death with such courage.
Dominie was arranging the time to bring Willem Communion on Sunday,
a sign *huisbezoek* was almost over.

"Dominie, you don't need to bring no Communion.
I feel the communion of the saints right here in bed.
I'll pray for you during the service.
But you can't move it away from where the saints are,
all together and Jesus with them,
and still keep it Communion.
Thanks for the idea, but don't bother."

He turned to me.
"And about the budget.
I pay, sure, but I envy them Israelites.
Priests ate a little of them unblemished lambs,
but the rest got burned up, useless to everybody but God.
All my budget money is an investment.
My Nelly was in our hospital and I'm in our Home.
All five children went to our Christian Schools,
four to our college.
Pete got a job with the Mission Board because he knows languages.
Bert took up business. Now he's on Synod's budget committee.
Lenore teaches philosophy at our college.
Jake is a preacher.
Now their children are in college and guess what?
They all want jobs like it.
I try to give my money to God, but none of it seems to get through.
Some year our churches ought to collect our money as usual,
put all the money on a boat in Muskegon Harbor,
set out for the middle of the lake,
and while Synod sings a psalm and prays on a boat near by,
sink the boat with the money on it
right to the bottom of Lake Michigan."

We left abruptly.
Dominie could think of nothing to pray
but the Lord's Prayer.

On Sunday at Communion
I remembered Willem was praying for us.

The cash in the offering of thanksgiving never looked greener
or colder.
Would the offertory prayer bury the green and cold of the cash
in the green and cold ocean of God's forgetfulness?
Would the offertory prayer transubstantiate the cash
into warm and living offering?

My style shattered,
I craved Willem's class.

# *Taking Death in Stride*
*(for Irene)*



When the *Sioux Center News* came on Thursdays,
Dad read Mother the three obituaries first.
Families in trade had their obituaries on the front page,
farmers like us on page two.
Wars and politics followed on pages five and six.

Each obituary got an amateur homily from Dad:

> "Bert de Barster was Christian Reformed,
> but I have my doubts that he died
> with his budget paid up."
>
> "Nelly Pinkster might have been a little narrow-minded,
> Protestant Reformed, you know,
> but we don't need to worry about her."
>
> "Imagine! Gary van Naven, dead under a train
> at seventeen. We'll send ten dollars
> to the First Reformed Mission Society.
> I'll send a note
> for his parents to take comfort
> in the doctrine of the Covenant."

Occasionally, an obituary appeared
for somebody without a Dutch name:

> "O O O their name is Gausewitz
> and their boy was killed on a motorcycle.
> Funeral in the Lutheran church,
> ja, but who's to say how serious they are?
> And not even the doctrine of the Covenant
> for his parents to take comfort in."

"Old man Perkins died.
I called him down once for swearing.
Hated me then, but may be thanking me now.
Mass on Saturday, but can we really go?
The Catechism says it is an accursed idolatry."

"Gorman from the old threshing ring died.
Never went to church and wouldn't hear talk of it.
Never had a better neighbor, though.
We'll go to the funeral, but I don't envy the minister
if he says what needs saying."



To Grand Rapids once they came
where the front page of the daily *Press*
was a boiling cauldron of unholy hatreds.
All week long
they turned immediately to the obituaries:
fifteen a day!

Twelve a day had either Polish
or German or Swedish
or Jewish or Italian or Black or English names
with corresponding funerals.

Three a day had Dutch names,
but three a day is too many to do homilies on,
especially if you don't know the people.
The folks recognized the names
of some of the officiating clergymen
and celebrated the orthodoxy of the denomination
in which these brothers and sisters had died.

There were three during the week
who had Dutch names with an un-Reformed funeral.
These rated a homily:

"De Gruyter. But no funeral.
Immediate cremation.
Ashes sprinkled over Lake Michigan.
What are they afraid of?"

"van Zwemeren, Catholic funeral.
Married Catholic, I guess.
Still, we can build on the doctrine of the Covenant."



"de Jongster. An organist, it says,
but Lutheran. I hope he didn't sell his Reformed birthright
for a musical mess of pottage."

On the fifth day of their visit,
as Dad and Mother retreated with the *Press*
to the dining room for their funeral rituals,
I told you, dear, of my embarrassment and anger:

"Why can't Dad and Mother take death in their stride?"

"Has it occurred to you," you said,
"that they are taking death in their stride?
Cities ignore death, but for an individual
is any calamity worse than death?
Maybe obituaries ought to be on the front page
and wars and floods in Section F.
Dad's reaching out to the dead in his little sermons
gives their dying some dignity for me."

Then, I could not tell my country parents
to exchange their style of death for the city's.
I was struck dumb, dear, by your class.

# *Home Grown*
*(for Chad and Eva Walsh)*

Whatever feels foreign away from home is style. 

The first night away from Middleburg and in Grand Rapids
Dad and Mother slept badly.

The first evening Dad said, "How odd
to be sleeping twenty miles from Lake Michigan.
And on the map I counted more than a hundred lakes
right around here—sure ain't Iowa."
Next morning Mother reported: "Dad and I
remembered Bell Lake last night,
just a mile west of Middleburg.
They tiled it off when we was kids."
Dad added: "That lake bottom
really made good farmland.
Don't you ever tile any of these off?"

The first evening Dad said, "Look
at all the sprinklers! Are they really necessary?
Even if gardens go brown one week, with all this rain,
they'd green right back up the next."
Next morning Mother reported: "Dad and I
remembered old Cornelia last night.
Always had the fanciest gardens in Middleburg.
Day lilies, dahlias, and hollyhocks,
all of them big as dinner plates
and her secret was watering every day."
Dad added: "Ja, and with buckets.
We didn't have running water then."

The first evening Dad said, "How funny
to ride mile after mile and never see a cornfield."
But the next afternoon we picked fruit in my friend's orchard
and Mother gave Dad a bigger peach than either of them had ever seen.
"Imagine," Mother said, "home grown!"—
as though she had looked out into her Middleburg cornfield
and found it had metamorphosed into a Michigan orchard
while her back was turned.
Dad bit into the raw peach with the same relish
he used for the first cooked and buttered roasting ears
every summer at home.



Where they went now there is no more sea
but I hope for a reclaimed seabed to remind them of the Bell Lake farms.
Among the unfamiliar flowers of Paradise
I hope for an occasional day lily, dahlia, or hollyhock
to remind them of Cornelia's garden.
And when Mother picks Dad the exotic fruit from the tree of life,
I hope she remembers to say: "Imagine! Home grown!"

Because to be at home away from home is class.

# LETTING THE TERMS GO

*Overheard after a* Style and Class *Reading*

"To put the labels *style* and *class*
in every single piece
is style.
Class
would let us figure some out
for ourselves."

# *26 June 1982*



Queen Beatrix was planting a sugar maple at Calvin College.

Pieter van Kampen, immigrant groundsman at the college
on the eve of his retirement,
was to help her plant the tree
to crown his career.

A mound of earth stood ready
next to the partially planted maple.

The queen was handed a ceremonial shovelful.
Everybody expected her to sprinkle it round the tree
and to declare the tree planted.
Then van Kampen was to shovel the rest of the mound.

But the queen proceeded to move the whole mound,
shovelful after shovelful,
and van Kampen said:
"Your Majesty,
the idea was that I would do something with you."

The royal reply:
"My shoes are not right for stamping the earth down
tight against the tree.
You do that."

# *Truth*



Sietze,
what you said about Queen Wilhelmina
and the Frisian Cattle Breeders' Association
is also told about Queen Victoria
and Yorkshire shepherds.
Did it happen twice?
Does every country tell it about its own queen?
Shall we write to Zoestdijk?
Shall we write to Buckingham Palace?
Shall we verify?
Shall we add a footnote?
Surely you can't go to print and not be sure.

> But suppose we checked
> and it turned out to be Victoria.
> The hair on my arm would not stand out
> as it did when I first heard the story
> about Wilhelmina—
> it will never stand out again on my arm
> for this story.
> To make it true for you
> I must be true to how I first heard it,
> to how I believed it happened,
> when the hair stood out on my arm.
>
> When Beatrix planted the tree,
> I was there!

Even if you were there,
how do we know you are telling the truth?

# *An Open Letter*

*(to Duane Bajema and Henry de Vries of the Department of Agriculture, Dordt College, Sioux Center, Iowa)*

Dear Duane and Henry: 

This letter is about your new Dordt farm.
My father is my sole credential for writing.
I lost my farmer's voice twenty years ago.
Eighty acres of Siouxland out of West Branch Valley,
my birthright, was then sold at public auction—
my third-generation homestead exchanged for cash.
My credential for writing, as I said, is my father,
as proud a farmer as ever farmed in Siouxland
in blue bib-overalls and black-striped tie,
as proud a farmer as ever farmed *op gereformeerde grondslag.*

Dad's first commandment was "Watch out for Ames"
and last commandment, too, and Ames included
all book-taught veterinarians, no matter where—
but not Kees Mouw, who never went to school.
Kees carried his bottles in a Rockford sock
and always took a swig of the medicine himself
from the Coke bottle in which he'd mixed it,
saying, "I reckon the old girl can stand this,"
before he poured it down the ailing cow.
Mouw was not Ames at all, but Ames included
all politicians after the farm vote, from the left
and right; all bureaucrats, whether from the United States
Department of Agriculture or the County Agent's office;
all salesmen of mineral supplements for hogs
except, of course, Henry Hulstein, who sold Peet's Perfection Minerals.

Now weed commissioners, even if they were our friends, were Ames.
The Farm Bureau and milking-machine salesmen were Ames.
*The Hoard's Dairyman* from Wisconsin was even more Ames
than *The Capper's Farmer* from Kansas. In 1940
the Department of Agriculture clear out in Washington
sent Dad a book of more than a thousand pages
called *Soils and Men.* It seems the county agent
had reported higher up that Dad raised flax.
The county agent thought our flax was his idea,
but Dad raised flax because his dad raised flax
for linseed oil and linen back in Friesland.
The book's concern was erosion. It urged contour farming.
Dad burned the book because it was from Ames
though its Washington postmark was in my stamp collection.
Ames was to Dad the whore of Babylon.
The Bible was his text for farming as for life.
For him it read: "Beware, beware of Ames!"

Into the daily swill of skim milk and cornmeal
Dad stirred an extra number-two canful
of Peet's Perfection Mineral Supplement
on Saturday nights for the pigs' Sunday breakfast.
It always foamed over the barrel by Sunday morning
and turned so crusty on top you had to cut it with a spade.
It was like slopping the pigs on Sunday with coffee cake.
Roy, Bob, Frank, and Snoodles, our four horses,
each got an extra gallon of oats on Sunday morning;
every cow an extra half-gallon of shelled-corn meal;
the chickens an extra gallon of shelled corn on the ground.
What would Ames have said of it if Ames had heard?
Ames has statistics probably that prove that
force-feeding hogs and cows one day in seven
does not step up hog growth or cow lactation.
Not even during threshing did our overweight horses
*need* extra oats, although they gladly feasted.
Only the chickens scorned the proffered banquet.
All summer long the chicken yard sprouted corn
left over from those Sunday morning feedings.
Can Ames ever comprehend Dad's explanations:

"We look to God as animals look to us.
We're their idea of God, their image of God.
God's love to animals flows through us to them.
How will they know God's love unless we show them?
How can they tell the Lord's Day from another?
How can we comfort animals except by food?
They groan for eternal sabbath with all creation."

Our problem, of course, was how to comfort Dad,
groaning more than his animals for eternal sabbath.
Dad knew from Zechariah that even horsebells
would read HOLINESS TO THE LORD at the final sabbath,
and if horsebells, then certainly corn planters
(except that Dad's excellent check was never perfect),
and if corn planters, then cultivators, too
(except that the patch of Russian thistles
could never be handled by even the best cultivator
and needed doctoring with salt and kerosene),
and if the corn machinery, then threshing machines
(except the settling up was never quite fair:
some wives had not had the ring over for dinner;
some neighbors borrowed horses to go out threshing;
some hayracks held only half as many bundles as others).
Nothing was ever good enough, even at Dad's best.
Yet some day every implement—every binder, hay rake,
corn knife, pinchers, whetstone, axe, and sledge
would read HOLINESS TO THE LORD.

The Dordt farm brings that day a little closer
when HOLINESS TO THE LORD is on every hog ring,
when every tractor, combine, and grain elevator
reads HOLINESS TO THE LORD;
when every milker, cooler, and sperm refrigerator
reads HOLINESS TO THE LORD;
when every roost, and nest, and incubator
reads HOLINESS TO THE LORD.

This letter is a welcome, Duane and Henry,
into the great tradition of Siouxland farming
self-consciously pursued *op gereformeerde grondslag,*
self-consciously pursued in Christian hope.

Do not despair if God's day should be slow in coming.
You wouldn't be the first generation to be disappointed.
Your waiting then makes a pattern, a tradition,
which you can pass intact to children's children
when today's Dordt farm comes to look as laughable
as my father's style of farming looks to me.
Then the pattern still stands and is not laughable.

I do not recommend Dad's barnyard sabbath;
overfeeding is overfeeding, even for God's sake.
Then, Duane and Henry, find some better methods—
but just as physical and free from greed—
to tell your animals God loves them through you.

Dad only ever burned one book I know of
and it was one too many: *Soils and Men*
might just have argued him into contour farming,
and cultivating less, and saving topsoil.
I hurt to say, as Dad would hurt to hear it:
in burning *Soils and Men,* Dad was not Reformed;
and in his fear of Ames, Dad was not Reformed.

In his fear of aping Ames, Dad *was* Reformed.
We need Ames, not to ape, but to evaluate
and then to follow what we judge consistent:
Ames brews insecticides that kill the birds
that are our chief defense against the insects;
concocts new fertilizers that nourish plants
but poison lakes and streams and shallow wells;
develops and destroys—and then deplores.
Ames needs a conscience and consistency.
Henry and Duane, do not be afraid of Ames—
a fearful conscience is, in fact, no conscience—
nor waver when Ames finds Dordt's farming purpose
as quaint as Dad's, because it is the same:
to keep eternal Sabbath on God's Homestead
with HOLINESS TO THE LORD on every milk pail.

**Do not take my word for it—I sold out.**
**But take my father's word. I hear him say it:**
**"You are not Ames. Dordt is not Ames. Watch out for Ames!"**

*op gereformeerde grondslag,*

Sietze Buning



*read at the Reformation Day Commemoration, 31 October 1980)*

# *The Consistorial Conference*

*(for Henie)*



In 1936, the summer of the drought,
Kuik, a janitor, Anton and Willem, retired farmers,
and Watse and Dad, farmers—
all elders in various Christian Reformed Churches—
organized the First Consistorial Conference
for all elders and deacons in the community
and also past elders and deacons
since those chosen once are likely to be chosen again.

The purpose was to define the offices of elder and deacon
without help from clergymen.
If clergy came, they would be guests.

There was to be one such meeting a year—
like classis without clergy—
and laymen were to read papers on subjects like
"The Purpose and Practice of *Censura Morum,*"
"Fair and Unfair Appraisals of Sermons,"
and "Excommunication in Reformed Perspective."

Planning the first meeting for October
required an afternoon meeting of the founders
in our living room on a July afternoon.

Listening from the kitchen,
Mother, Auntie, Klaas, and I
heard Kuik's voice addressing God
as if God were a public meeting very well attended,
and then all five voices joined in on the Genevan Psalm 135.
The psalm could not have been more properly pitched to the occasion
if it had been a solemn consistory at the Vatican,
all about office-bearers in the House of God,
but it was an unfamiliar melody,
none of the five played the piano,
and none of the five had a disciplined ear.
A strange six-part cacophony came from the parlor—
six-part, because we forgot to shoo Snoeky, our mongrel, outside
and when the melody went high in the fourth line,
Snoeky joined in with an obbligato.
When the psalm was over, my mother's cue,
she could not serve the cake and coffee for laughter.
She made Klaas and me do it.

One Founders' Meeting was enough to plan the meeting in 1936,
but two planning sessions were necessary in 1937—
already it was getting harder to find topics—
and during the third year
there was a meeting in every founder's parlor,
five before the next October.
Right after New Year they began planning for October.

We could tell by listening from the kitchen
when the meeting was at our house
that gradually Watse was becoming the leader.
His voice was heard more frequently without interruption.
After meetings Dad would have *Om Nabij God te Zijn,*
one or another of the three volumes of *Pro Rege,*
or an old issue of *De Standaard,* the newspaper—
all written or edited by Abraham Kuyper
and all with Watse's name inscribed in them.

The issue at the annual meetings of the Consistorial Conference
increasingly became "The Need for a Calvinistic
University in America." "Not a place, first of all,"
Dad would explain at dinner, echoing Watse,
"to award degrees and certify teachers—
we have Calvin, and Hope, and Central, and Northwestern to do that,
and a hundred Lutheran and Methodist colleges to boot,
and who shall say how many Catholic schools—
but a finer university even than Kuyper's
Free University of Amsterdam,
claiming the whole universe for the Kingdom of Christ."



My brother and I said in bed:
"Isn't Watse making Dad weird?
You need a man like Einstein for a university,
or a man like F. Melius Christiansen,
or a man like Abraham Kuyper.
Who do these farmers think they are, planning a university?"

When Watse Bierma died in 1940 my brother had left home
and Mother asked me to skip school on the day of the funeral:
"We may have a time with Dad."

We did.
Dad was disconsolate between Mother and me,
the first time I had seen him disconsolate.

On the way to the cemetery he said,
"I'm sad for Watse Bierma.
There can't ever be the university now either."
And I thought, but did not say, "Foolish, foolish man!"

But put the case that somebody should ask me today
why there is no Calvinistic University in America
and I will answer with conviction:
"Because Watse Bierma died in 1940."
His urgency for a Calvinistic university
was as rare a gift as Einstein's.

# *Election*



Nobody would tell who had written the naughty word
inside the door of the boys' toilet.

The six girls in our one-room country school
were dismissed, and the five boys—
two older and two younger than I,
and I in fifth grade—were left behind.

"Write on a piece of paper," the teacher said,
"the name of the person you think did it,
put the paper on your inkwell,
and put your head down on your desk."

Teacher's footsteps from desk to desk,
the unfolding of paper,
and afterwards:
"Sietze,
you will stay to write five-hundred times
'I will be pure in thought, word, and deed.' "

Elected but not guilty,
I ran home, the copying done,
and cried in outrage.

"But who," said Dad, "put the tiddlywinks
in the collection plate on Sunday?
The deacons found them
and they're missing from your set."

So much for outraged innocence.

"Poor teacher," said Dad,
"what can she do with lying
foulmouthed boys?
No wonder she makes mistakes."

So much for my mistrial.

"And now you know," Dad said,
"a very little bit about how Jesus felt
being punished for sins he didn't do."

So much for self-pity.

Dad gave me the tiddlywinks from his overall pocket:
"I'll see the teacher, though.
Whoever did it shouldn't get away with it."

Next day my friend Ted was washing the toilet wall.

"Hey, how did your dad know I did it?"

To this day
I do not know how he knew.

# *Telling it Straight*



Sietze,
we were with Queen Juliana the whole day
when she was at Calvin College,
and no professor, old or otherwise,
commented on the size of her legs.

I never said it was Calvin College.
I said it was a campus that shall go unnamed.
Everybody thought it was Calvin.

Where did it happen, then?

I can't remember.
The person who first told me the story is dead.
He might have said the University of Utrecht.
I seem to remember Utrecht.
Though maybe it didn't happen at a university at all.
Maybe someone on a street in a village commented on her legs.

Sietze, Sietze,
why don't you find out where it happened,
if at all, and tell it straight?

Because an American audience tunes out
when it hears Utrecht.

So you admit you say it happened at Calvin?

No, I have only ever said that it happened
at a campus that shall go unnamed,
although—

Although what?

Although,
when I read it aloud for people,
if there is no laughter of recognition at that line,
usually I add a line like this:

Let me only say it was not Dordt College.

After that line everybody always laughs.

You leave a false impression.

I must, to make it true.

Your story sounds like a pack of lies to me.

But when Beatrix planted the tree
I was there!

But how do we know you are telling anything straight?

# A TALE OF TWO TOWNS

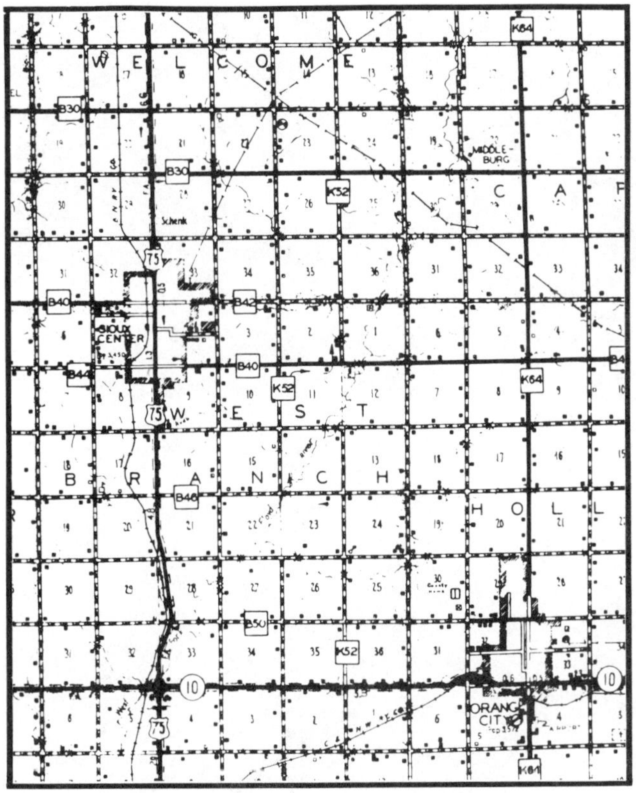

# *A Tale of Two Towns*



## 1. *Difference*

The difference between Sioux Center and Orange City
was not yet clear to me at six,
the winter we were snowbound, 1936,
nor had I seen the difference between both towns
and Middleburg.
Town was where you got candy.

We were snowbound for a whole month after the new year.
Klaas almost died of smallpox.
The doctor made it through to name what ailed him
but couldn't get back with medicine.

Ropes led Dad from house to barn
and he needed to shovel paths every day
to lead cows and horses to the watering tank
one at a time.

Mother and Aunty butchered chickens
(chicken soup was all Klaas wanted),
chopped wood, and fetched apple baskets full of corncobs
(to keep the cookstove and the base burner going through the night),
and washed (Klaas's bedding needed changing every day).

Nobody had time for me, and I was desperate.
Until the paper ran out, I drew pictures of houses,
all alike except for the color
and whether or not they had window boxes.
Over each house I put a motto:
HOME SWEET HOME,
GOD BLESS OUR HOME,
PRAYER CHANGES THINGS, and
JESUS NEVER FAILS.

The very day the paper ran out,
the smallpox and the snowstorm stopped together,
the sun was shining, and I asked Dad
to take me to town for a nougat bar,
our broad term for Baby Ruth, Mars, and Mr. Goodbar.

"We can't go out for nougat bars," Dad said.
"The sun may be shining, but the roads are still blocked."

"Then I'll walk," I said.



"Four miles? A little better?"

"Sure."

"Where will you get money?"

"I saved some."

In the house I emptied my bank,
a dollar's worth in pennies and nickels,
and I set out for Middleburg, struggling
up and over the snowbanks, twice as high as I was.

I made it to the corner, when I heard Dad's voice:

"Sietze, Sietze."
He was calling from the farmyard.

I turned back.
They must have decided to drive to town.
I took no time at all getting back.

"Are we going to town?"

"No, Sietze, we can't go
today. But it's too cold and you're too little
to walk better than four miles by yourself."

I said nothing, but in a rage
I flung the dollar's worth of useless pennies and nickels
into a bare cottonwood tree next to the house,
burst into tears, ran inside,
and hid under the bed of the patient getting better,
in the living room next to the base burner.

When Dad came in with a handful of change
for Mother to put in my bank,
he did not laugh and he did not scold,
and he suggested a taffy pull for me that evening.
I remember that taffy pull.

I also remember that I had been on my way to Middleburg
where we went to church—
not on my way to Orange City or Sioux Center.

Six is the last time I remember
choosing Middleburg over Orange City and Sioux Center
or considering it equal.

### 2. *The Tie*

By seven I understood that during the week
I could wear the same bib-overall and blue shirt
to Orange City, Sioux Center, or Middleburg,
and a suit, white shirt, and tie to all three places
Sundays.



By seven I also understood that Dad was different:
Sundays
he wore a suit, white shirt, and tie all three places
just as I did.
During the week
he wore the same bib-overall he slopped the pigs with
with blue shirt and tie
to Middleburg,
a new bib-overall
with blue shirt and tie
to Sioux Center,
but he wore pressed trousers with a belt
with a white shirt with a black fleck in it
(*wit met zwarte stip*)
to Orange City,
with, of course, a tie.

The only garment he wore to all three towns was the tie.

### *3. Other Clothes*

By eight
I realized Mother's fashions for shopping
followed Dad's.
She did not change her cotton housedress
to shop in Middleburg,
changed to a clean cotton housedress
to shop in Sioux Center,
and changed into a cast-off Sunday silk dress
to shop in Orange City.

## *4. Friendly or Proper?*



By nine
I realized my parents greeted everybody in Middleburg
because they knew everybody there,
greeted everybody in Sioux Center
whether they knew them or not,
but in Orange City
greeted only the people they knew.

"Why dress up to shop in Orange City and not in Sioux Center?"
"Why greet everybody in Sioux Center and not in Orange City?"

"Sioux Center is friendly and Orange City is proper."

"Which one is better?"

Dad: "Orange City."
Mother: "Sioux Center."

## 5. *Tattling*

At ten
I knew that teenagers from Orange City tattled
and teenagers from Sioux Center never did.

A dozen older boys from Sioux Center
including my brother
decided to run away from home.
My brother, it turned out later,
was the first to decide against it.
Gradually others dropped out.
At last only two were left:
a grocer's son and a pastor's son.
They left as scheduled on the first of March
and were gone only a month or so.
Only after they returned did we know
that ten others had been involved,
had backed out,
had been in touch with the runaways by telephone
all the while they were in Minneapolis,
and had even been up to see them in Minneapolis.
Only after they returned did we know.

The pastor said:
"How cruel not to tell us what you knew."
The grocer said:
"Didn't you know we never slept once during that whole month?"
The pastor said:
"Didn't you know we were crying at every meal?"
The grocer said:
"Didn't you know my wife had a nervous breakdown from it?"
The prodigal sons were embraced
and the non-tattlers were accused.
The only explanation the non-tattlers gave:
"This isn't Orange City."

The summer before a fishing party from Orange City,
five men and a boy,
got lost on some connected lakes in Minnesota.
They rowed up to shore expecting to find their camp
only to find desolate woods,
so they tramped and explored and got worried—
and got thirsty—
and then they found a cabin in the woods,
open,
and there were six warm beers on a shelf.
Somebody said, "Let's leave some money
and drink the beers."
The men all drank.
The boy said nothing but refused the beer,
thirsty as he was.
Refreshed,
the others figured out that they were on the wrong lake,
so they rowed back into the original lake,
found their camp,
and were happy—
all but the boy.

He fumed with outrage all the way back to Orange City
and he told his mother how much beer each man had drunk
including the boy's father,
and the mother and son went straight to the three ministers
of the five men (and two of them elders even)
and told how much beer each man had drunk
and what a bad example they all had been for the boy.

So that was why the non-tattlers from Sioux Center
said, "This isn't Orange City,"
when the parents of the prodigals accused them of not tattling.

The non-tattlers from Sioux Center said to us,
though not to the parents of the prodigals:
"Suppose we had told where the runaways were?
That two boys ran away is only a sign of a corruption
so deep in Sioux Center that nobody knows the limit.
What made all of us want to run away?
What made some of us decide against it?
Are we to blame for not running or for planning to run at first?
Are the prodigals to blame for running or for coming back?
Are our parents less to blame than the parents of the runaways?
Are our parents to blame for being glad we didn't run,
or to blame for making Sioux Center the kind of place
some of us would gladly run from?
What's wrong with Sioux Center is so deep
that telling where the runaways were
wouldn't have solved anything."



Orange City was all agreed
that the tattling mother and son had shown great courage:
"If only we clear up some of this beer-snitching
and set a little better example for the youth,
Orange City won't have a whole lot wrong with it."

I was only beginning to study the doctrine of total depravity
with Gerben Zylstra in Middleburg.
I knew all Calvinists confessed it,
both in Orange City and Sioux Center,
but it seemed to me that Sioux Center
had the more practical understanding of the dogma.

## *6. Goat*

My cousin in Orange City was eleven, just like I was.
The difference between us was that I merely liked animals,
having so many pets to choose from on the farm.
He was always totally smitten with one or another animal
he couldn't keep in town.

We were together in the salebarn in Orange City.
A goat came into the ring,
and my cousin wanted it more than he had ever wanted any animal.
The auctioneer couldn't get a bid.
Again and again he said,
"What'll you offer me for this goat?
The owner must sell. Moving to California tomorrow.
What am I bid?"
Wilbur hollered,
"Two bits,"
hoping somebody else would bid
and hoping just as hard that nobody else would.

Nobody else did.
After the sale Wilbur went to the office to pay his quarter,
trying not to imagine what would happen
when the stock truck stopped at Uncle Dewey's house
right across from Bronkema's church.

Well, that goat never even got off the truck.
"We can't have a goat," Aunt Alice said.
"He'll sneak into the house and eat the curtains."

"We can't have a goat," Uncle Dewey said.
"He'll eat all my young trees."

"You can't have a goat," Dominie Bronkema said.
"He will bleat during prayers."

"I won't let him.
I'll train him.
I'll watch him.
I'll keep him on a leash.
I'll teach him not to bleat during prayers," Wilbur said.

But everybody agreed Orange City was no place for a goat.

## 7. *Salebarns*



We needed cats on our farm to keep mice down and rats away.
No cat came into the house.
Some skim milk in the cat pan was all the care they got.
They were fruitful and multiplied
but farm catastrophes kept the cat population in line.
A few were kicked by cows and stepped on by horses,
others were ground down by wagon wheels and smothered under hay,
and one white, black, and orange one
got run over by the cream hauler.

When I was twelve the cat population got out of hand.
Dad and I tied our jacket sleeves tight against our wrists
and our overall cuffs tight against our ankles
with binder twine
and caught a dozen.
We put three cats to a gunnysack
and took four sacks to the Sioux Center salebarn.

After the shorthorn heifers,
after the bulls, the milch cows, and the calves,
after the boars, the ponies, and so much more—
it is impossible to say just how insignificant
the four sacks of cat looked
or how rank the cats' fear was throughout the salebarn.
"Sam Buning is selling cats in bags," said the auctioneer.
Laughter.
Fred Krommendyk from Hull said he'd pay a dollar for a bag,
but he wanted to see them first.

"Look at your own risk," Dad said.

Somebody snipped the sack open
and three terrified cats fizzed out like rootbeer,
white fur bristling.
When Fred Krommendyk reached to pick one up,
the critter laid Fred's arm open with his claws
and then streaked after his brother and sister
into the rafters, a blur of white, black, and orange.

"You can't catch them now," Dad said.
Fred Krommendyk got a new sack, closed this time,
and somebody from South Dakota got the other two sacks.
The first three cats made themselves at home in the salebarn.

Weeks later I was back in the salebarn,
and there were our cats still,
all three,
up in the rafters, down in the ring,
among the buyers,
at home,
making free.



"Dad, look at our cats."

"Ja, our cats all right."

"Dad, what do they live on?"

"Rats, mice, leftovers from Marie's lunchroom."

"Does the salebarn just let them live here?"

"Sure. This isn't Orange City salebarn.
In Orange City some deadeye would have come with a .22 rifle
and clipped all three off."

"Aren't you glad we brought our cats
to the Sioux Center salebarn and not Orange City?"

"You forget, Sietze, that I'm an Orange City boy.
I'm kind of a deadeye myself."

I did remember
all the dinners of pheasant and cottontail,
all shot in the head with Dad's .22.

"And why didn't you shoot our cats at home then
with our .22?"

"Your mother wouldn't have liked it.
But nobody else ever brings cats to a salebarn.
If you gotta bring cats to a salebarn, though,
bring 'em to Sioux Center.
They'll laugh at you in Orange City."

And I realized I was as much Sioux Center as Orange City,
my mother as my father,
and if Wilbur had bought his goat in Sioux Center,
somebody would have found a way
for him to take care of his goat in the salebarn.

## *8. Bargains*

By thirteen I realized
why my mother preferred to shop in Sioux Center,
my father in Orange City.

The clerks in Sioux Center stores
were hired at random from the community.

The clerks in Orange City stores were children of the owners,
themselves scheduled to become owners.

The turnover in clerks was so fast in Sioux Center
that they didn't even learn your name
and you could shop anonymously.
Or if somebody stayed on and on,
like Allie at de Ruyter's Hardware,
you still assumed she was on your side against the owners.
You could say, "They sure don't make these
can openers the way they used to,"
without wondering whether she would tell George de Ruyter on you.
Or you could say,
"I'm returning this pocketknife.
The blade broke off
the first time Klaas pitched it like a dart at the corncrib."
This much Allie would report to George to get your money back,
but she wouldn't add that you had also said:
"We're going to send for a new knife from Sears.
We're thinking of sending for a new cream separator too."

The clerks in Orange City always knew you and your parents
generations back.
They either greeted you by name
or asked your name
and tied it in with all the relatives they knew on both sides
before they helped you
and they never forgot it afterwards.
And if you said, "That toaster you sold us is worthless.
It burns the toast. I would like my money back please,"
then the teenage daughter of the owner would say,
"Why, Mrs. Buning, it's the best toaster money can buy.
It's a beaut, Madam, a beaut,"
and if you persisted, the older brother would say,
"Isn't Mrs. Mellema your sister,
the one who returned a perfectly good percolator last week?"
and if you persisted, the owner himself would stroll over and say,
"Didn't I read in *The Capital*
your sister Minnie was visiting from Omaha?
Visiting Mrs. Mellema and you.
Now what am I to think?
Maybe that Mrs. Mellema usually drinks boiled coffee
and that you toast bread over a corncob fire,
but because your sister Minnie was coming from the city
you and Mrs. Mellema wanted to serve her
perked coffee and toaster toast like she's used to.
I'm not saying it's how it is.
I'm just saying I might think that's how it is if you return it."
Mother always came home again from Orange City
with what she had set out to return.
She preferred shopping in Sioux Center.

Whenever Dad returned anything in Orange City,
he insisted on seeing the owner.
After the chitchat about crops and weather,
Dad would open negotiations something like this:
"Is it true that your brother Bill
was baptized for a second time in Lake Okoboji
by some strange minister named Smith or Brown?
It's all right, I guess, but I hate to see
the faith that our fathers suffered for
just stepped out of like a suit of clothes.
I have respect for this second baptism all right.
This Smith or Brown probably does a lot of good,
but I can't understand that he has so little respect—
and that Bill has so little respect—
for our baptism.
Why, I was the young elder who held the basin
when Bill was baptized as a baby. He was my first.
I also remember holding the basin for you.
Cute little tykes you both were.
And now I read in *The Capital* that you too went to Okoboji
to see this Smith or Brown or Russel or whatever his name is
baptize Bill and his family.
I sure hope that Baptist way doesn't look good to you."
All of it sincerely meant—though strategically placed,
for then came the afterthought:
"By the way, the pulleys in this here wire stretcher you sold me
aren't any good. The rope's fine, but the pulleys don't turn."
Dad left with new pulleys
won fair and square.

Dad felt guilty shopping in Sioux Center.
It was as though the customer and the clerk
were cheating behind the owner's back.

## 9. *More Bargains*



By fourteen I was a connoisseur of a good bargain.
Dad and I went to a farm sale south of Orange City
and we saw Old Graanstra drive the best bargain I have ever seen.

Old Graanstra was bidding against only one opponent
for his choice of one horse out of a team.
It was evident that one horse was much younger and friskier.
We all assumed that Old Graanstra was bidding on the better horse.

It was Old Graanstra's turn to bid
and he announced he would not raise his bid
unless the auctioneer took a break
so Old Graanstra could inspect the horses again.
Graanstra astounded everyone by inspecting the inferior horse:
opened his mouth to check his teeth
and swatted him on the rump to check his reflexes.
Then, yes, he would raise his bid, reluctantly.

The opponent did not raise the bid.
Why shouldn't he get the better horse as second choice
if Old Graanstra chose the inferior horse as first choice.
Except, when the auctioneer asked Old Graanstra for his choice,
he decided after all on the superior horse,
not the one he had taken time out to inspect.

The Orange City crowd murmured and laughed approval of Old Graanstra
and there was a patter of applause
though the opponent, of course, did not join in.
Dad shook Old Graanstra's hand.
It was like winning at chess.

A year later we were at a farm sale west of Sioux Center.
We were in the market for a new horse to take Bob's place
against Prince after Bob died during threshing time.
Dad assumed the same position Old Graanstra was in before.
He called time out to inspect the inferior horse,
the opponent ceased,
Dad was given his choice,
and he chose the superior horse.

But the Sioux Center crowd's silence was so ominous,
and the murmur that followed was so disapproving,
that Dad reversed his choice.
We ended up with the inferior horse.
A farm sale in Sioux Center is not a chess game.

## *10. Above the Mean*

What Dutchness is
first became clear to me
as I became aware of non-Dutchness.

What Sioux-Centerness is
and what Orange-Cityness is
became clear to me
by how each town handled non-Dutchness.

Marian Hospers,
wife of Willy Hospers of Sioux Abstract Company,
was from "out east" (we never knew from how far east),
had met Willy "at school" (we never knew which school),
and had sung in opera (we never knew which opera).

It was not necessary to know
since we did know that the year the Sioux County Farm Bureau
asked her to direct their Women's Chorus (1936)
was the year
when the Sioux County Farm Bureau Women's Chorus
sang at the World's Fair in New York
and got good notices in the New York papers.

It was not necessary to know where she was from
to know that she was quality.
She was the only lady in Sioux County
who kept her dining room table set at all times.
She was the only lady in Sioux County
who kept *Harpers*, *The Atlantic*, and *Saturday Review*
on her living room coffee table.
She was the only lady in Sioux County who went to Chicago
for the opera.
She was the only lady in Sioux County
who changed clothes for dinner every night—
a late dinner, and we could peek in
and get an idea of the clothes.

Still, she fit in.
She directed the choir in her Reformed Church.
She entertained her Reformed Dominie and his wife at dinner.
She sang for the community's Good Friday service.
She entertained the neighborhood ladies.
She taught a dozen students voice lessons
("No more than a dozen—it interferes with my personal life"),
one of whom was I,
from the time my voice changed until I left for college.

Marie Reviere,
wife of the editor of the *Sioux Center News,*
was from out east (we didn't know how far),
had met Ed at school (we didn't know which one),
and was a talented musician.

We knew.
There was a meeting of all families of servicemen
held in the Sioux Center Town Hall
sponsored by the *Sioux Center News.*
Klaas was in service, so we went.
Marie Reviere played the piano:
"Bluebirds Over the White Cliffs of Dover,"
"Put All Your Troubles in Your Old Kit Bag,"
"Tangerine,"
and other songs we only ever heard over the radio,
all played with honky-tonk pizzazz.

The following week
she was gathering ads from the merchants,
and I saw her go into vanden Berg's piano store,
and I followed her in,
and she whipped out the first movement
of Beethoven's Opus 10, number 2
from memory,
every appoggiatura, arabesque, and mordent in place,
the way I was trying to get the same sonata
studying with Maybelle Riemann in Hull.
And I said to Marie, "Will you teach me?"
and she said, hard and brittle,
"I work for the newspaper, kid."

Whenever I saw her, there was some frantic oddness:
I saw her collecting ads on roller skates,
in mink coat,
in swimming suit,
in turban,
in black tailored suit,
heavily made up,
without any makeup and with flecks of grey in her hair,
looking sixteen,
looking sixty,
always looking frantic.
I never dared to talk to her again,
too young at fifteen
to see how desperate she was.

Now and then there was a rumor:
Marie and the implement man,
Marie and the depot agent,
Marie and the local basketball star.
Marie and her husband finally left town.
It was more Sioux Center's failure than their own.

But then Marian Hosper's staying in Orange City happily
was as much Orange City's success as her own.

Landowners from Friesland gave Orange City its tone.
They expected any happy society to be organized in classes.
They knew instinctively how to accommodate an aristocrat.

Day laborers from Gelderland and Overijsel gave Sioux Center its tone.
They came to America for a classless society.
They suspected Marie of putting on airs.
They only half-consciously froze her out of town.

## *11. Competence*

Compare John Marra, the incompetent,
and Moley, the dwarf.

Orange City was cruel to John Marra
and Sioux Center to Moley.



Always the relentless teasing by the young
learned from their elders,
and sometimes physical abuse:

> Asking John Marra
> "Why is the depot at the south end of town
> and not on main street?"
> and howling with laughter when he answered
> "Because the trains come in at the south end."
>
> Scaring John Marra because he scared so well,
> always sure he was dying of it this time.
>
> Getting two beers down Moley
> and taking him to the Baptist's baptism
> at Sandy Hollow
> to hear Moley prophesy against adult baptism
> from the hood of a Model A.
>
> Getting two beers down Moley
> and then leaving him indecently exposed
> at the entrance to de Ruyter's Hardware
> until the cop tucked him in.

John Marra made birdhouses,
carved with pictures of Indians and tulips.
Anybody who could make birdhouses as well as that
and carve pictures as well as that
could have had some job:
        shining shoes at the very least,
        or sweeping floors,
        or making packing crates.
Some people treated him kindly enough,
but nobody saw to it that he had a steady job.



Moley was a harness maker and shoemaker.
For years he worked for Willem van Steenwijk.
As long as he worked, he made harnesses.
Horses were fewer and fewer,
but so were experienced harness makers.
Trade finally came from a hundred miles away
for Moley to make harnesses.

Moley had his place on the revolving stools at Central Cafe.
He was no loiterer, even as a retiree.
He looked you straight in the eye.
How people treated him didn't even matter that much
because he was somebody.

Sioux Center, which could not accommodate Marie, accommodated Moley.
Orange City, which could accommodate Marian Hospers,
could not accommodate John Marra.

John Marra always went neatly clothed,
but clothing is not the chief problem among South African blacks
either.

John Marra was never hungry,
but hunger is not the chief problem of Vietnamese refugees in San Francisco
either.

John Marra was never sent home from church,
but being sent home from church is not the chief problem of the ex-convict
either.

It would be hard going in Sioux County
if I were Black, or Vietnamese, or an ex-convict,
but I would rather take my chances in Sioux Center than in Orange City.

## 12. *Two Dykstras*



The summer I turned fifteen
I joined the sellout crowd at the Orange City Town Hall,
and even went to the dress rehearsal the night before,
to see *Het Spul Draait,*
a play on the life of Galileo,
every word of it in Frisian.

The Reverend B.D. Dykstra wrote it,
produced it, directed it,
and starred in it.

It was less about Galileo, the seventeenth-century Italian,
than about Broer Doekeles Dykstra,
the twentieth-century American-Frisian.

The story was Galileo's silencing by the church.
The Grand Inquisitor,
Pete De Vries the Supervisor,
showed Galileo the instruments of torture,
and thundered at him.
BD cringed.
The inquisitor offered to ignore the instruments of torture
if Galileo and his daughter,
played by Agnes Te Paske, BD's sister,
would willingly submit to house arrest
and give up their experiments in astronomy.
Everyone knew those experiments contradicted the Scriptures:
Galileo's experiments established that the world is round;
the Scriptures establish that the earth has four corners.

BD, like Galileo, had been silenced by the church.
He had been an outspoken pacifist during the First World War.
He had founded a Christian Academy in Harrison, South Dakota,
where all students would be expected to study Greek,
Latin, Dutch, German, French, English,
and, of course, Frisian.
English would be used only to study the other languages,
and subjects like math and geography
would be studied in foreign languages.

He did not bother to check with the State of South Dakota, of course,
whether he could be accredited.
It ought to be evident to anybody
that he was qualified to run the school.
It was a boarding school
for which Mrs. Dykstra did all the cooking
and the washing—by hand,
for there was no washing machine,
though there was a printing press.
How else could he get out his pamphlets against war?



Against war and against the education around him,
he seemed anti-American,
and so he was relieved of his congregation in South Dakota
and placed under a form of house arrest.
He was never again an active pastor,
but he served as stated clerk of classis,
occupied pulpits a Sunday at a time, and
edited *De Volksvriend*—
the Dutch language weekly.
There, under the pen name of Agricola,
he editorialized against war and for the simple life.
If Roosevelt, Hoover, Churchill, and Hitler
each tended his own acre of ground the way it ought to be tended—
the way BD tended his own acre, overrun with greenery—
they would all be too busy to declare war on each other.
If they all avoided motor cars—
BD only ever rode happily on a bicycle or train—
nobody would be available to drive a jeep or tank.

This radical pacifist played Galileo in his play,
the pacifist's non-pacifist sister Agnes played his daughter,
and we had Americans playing Italians in the Frisian language.

Even under house arrest, the historical Galileo would have drunk wine.
No inquisitor would have withheld it from the most notorious heretic.
Even if it had been a Frisian play in Friesland,
Galileo would have drunk wine.
Not from their Reformed heritage, but from American Protestantism,
the Dykstras had learned to avoid wine.

Agnes was the founder of Sioux Center's WCTU.
Every June she gave a party for the town's new babies
and for their mothers.
Each baby had a blue or pink ribbon tied around its finger,
a sign that the child would not touch strong drink.

Agnes and BD were united in their love of the Frisian language
and in their American abhorrence of alcohol,
though BD would gladly have made some accommodation
for the sake of the play:
"It needn't be a drink, Agnes, just the illusion of a drink,
just enough to give Galileo the look of an Italian."
Agnes would have none of it.



Agnes admired Galileo, admired her brother,
but shared none of her brother's annoyance with the establishment.
Her husband was the mayor of Sioux Center.
It never even occurred to her
that BD's story was Galileo's.
Sioux Center's first lady was teaching the community
what wholesome entertainment is.

On the face of it both Dykstras were in the wrong town.
Agnes, the aristocratic moralist,
should have lived in Orange City,
where you dressed up properly to go to town
and greeted only the people you knew,
where the salebarn was kept tidy,
and where tattling helped to keep sinners in line.
BD, the pacifist and egalitarian,
the anti-materialist,
the Agricola of the *Volksvriend*
(as close to a Marxist rag as Sioux County will ever know)—
BD, our nonconforming Galileo,
belonged in Sioux Center.
For a long time I thought
both towns got the wrong Dykstra.

Suppose BD had lived in Sioux Center
where his ideas would have had a better chance to catch on.
The natural antinomianism of Sioux Center
could only have been aggravated by BD's presence.
Suppose everyone had ridden bicycles in defiance of the Industrial Revolution.
Suppose everyone had gone pacifist and run the American Legion out of town.
Suppose everyone had gone agrarian,
planting at least one living seed every day,
summer and winter,
their places overrun with greenery like BD's own.



Or suppose Agnes had held her annual WCTU tea in Orange City.
Orange City would have taken the vows and ribbons
as seriously as Confession of Faith.
The College Inn would have folded if Agnes had lived in Orange City,
whereas Doc's Cafe thrived in Sioux Center in spite of her.
Agnes was aunty to the whole town of Sioux Center,
and everybody took her party like any aunty's party,
seriously, with appreciation, and with a little condescension.
All the mothers knew that the blue-ribboned babies
would all become occasional patrons at Doc's Cafe.
Would you really want your sons to be brought up in Sioux Center
and never have been inside Doc's Cafe?
Of course, when you knew your son had been to Doc's
you worried that Agnes would find out,
because if she did,
your son would never be a Sunday School teacher
in any church in Sioux Center.
Agnes kept all pastors informed in all the churches,
and now and again kept consistories informed
about which ministers were seen at Doc's.

With BD in Sioux Center,
Sioux Center would be a militantly pacificist town by now.
With Agnes Dykstra Te Paske in Orange City,
Orange City would be a little to the right
of the John Birch Society by now.

That both towns have settled into an identical Republicanism
I take to be the dubious achievement of BD and Agnes,
each wearing down the extremes
in a town where each was an alien.
Each town got the right Dykstra,
not because they fit in so well,
but precisely because they did not.

And BD and Agnes
had the leads in BD's *Het Spul Draait,*
a life of Galileo in Frisian,
when I was fifteen.



I was there two nights.
My father was in tears at the end of the dress rehearsal,
and I wondered what I had missed
and went the next night again to find out why
and it's taken me all of these thirty-eight years
to come as close as I have.

## *13. Kees Mouw*

Sioux Center and Orange City were contrasts for me
before I left for college.
My first summer home after being away,
the whole county seemed remote.

In mid-June, soon after I arrived,
one of the cows broke into the young corn
and ate herself into a bloat.
She made it back into the pasture
but fell down outside the barn.
"It's too late for the vet," Dad said,
"We better get Kees Mouw."
We had ordered Kees Mouw before—
agnostic, widower, and self-taught animal doctor,
but he looked different to me this time:
the sorrel that drew his barouche had never looked so sleek,
the barouche had never looked so much like a chariot,
nor the long buggy whip in its holder so much like a plume.
He did not step but jumped down from his barouche
in spite of his eighty years.
He carried his medicines in three Rockford socks.
He saw the sick cow and let loose with an anathema:
*Verrekte kreng, jij bent een*
*Amsterdamsebijersbierbrouwerijmaatschapijaandeelhouwdersvrouwszuster.*
The cow did not respond to his healing word.

So he took an ordinary butcher knife out of one of the socks,
wiped both sides clean on his shirt,
and plunged it all the way to the hilt
between two ribs on the cow's back.
Some bubbly gas escaped, but not enough—
though for the first time the cow stirred.

Next Kees picked out some boxes of powders and bottles of potions
and using a funnel, poured a bit of each
into an empty Coke bottle—
funnel, boxes, bottles, and Coke bottle all coming out of the socks—
shook it all up into a brown foam,
stuck a finger in,
tasted,
and said: *"Dat kan de kreng wel staan."*
("The old sonofabitch can stand this.")



Kees knelt,
propped the thick animal-neck up on his own wirey thighs,
pried the teeth apart,
and poured the liquid down.
The smell was alarmingly medicinal.
I did not doubt the changes it would make in any critter's innards.

Kees packed up his equipment,
wiped the butcher knife on his shirt,
and sat down against the barn to wait for improvement.

In a half hour the cow was not improved.

So Kees ordered us to get the post auger
and he had us bore four holes for the cow's legs,
just deep enough so the cow's hooves
would not touch the bottom.

Kees, Dad, and I dragged the cow
and eased her legs into the holes.
The cow's belly pressed against the ground.

*"Kijk er niet na de hele dag,"*
Kees said.
*"Morgen is ze dood en er nog in,
of er uit en beter."*

("Don't look at this at all today,"
Kees said.
Of course not.
If the tame cow saw us,
she would expect us to ease her discomfort
and stop struggling.
"Tomorrow," Kees said,
"she will be dead and trapped
or alive and well and out.")

As we left, the cow was feebly struggling
against the discomfort.

It was about noon by now.
Kees stayed for dinner and kept his hat on
even during the prayers.
After dinner he went home
without stopping to check the cow.

And all of it was as foreign
to the life I had been living at college
as snake charming and faith healing.

That afternoon Dad and I went to Sioux Center.
The chief errand was getting a check from the Farmers' COOP Elevator
for a load of last year's oats,
trucked out to make room for this year's.
We also delivered eggs to the Farmers' COOP Produce,
got gas at the Farmers' COOP Service Station
and buttermilk at the Farmers' COOP Creamery.

On the way home, I brought it up:
"Why all the COOPs in Sioux Center, Dad?
A COOP Lumberyard, even a COOP Burial Association,
and all the others.
Why so few COOPs in Orange City?
And the COOP Filling Station is the smallest in Orange City?"

Dad seemed to change the subject:
"You saw what Kees Mouw did with our sick cow?
Kees Mouw is Orange City.
He never would have made it in Sioux Center.
Orange City figures that public demand can describe the job
and fix the fee.
If Kees Mouw didn't cure so many animals,
Orange City would have let him starve
or sent him to the poor farm.
Orange City doesn't care how odd Kees is,
as long as he cures sick animals.
Sioux Center will support only vets with diplomas.
Sioux Center—great at giving everybody a fair deal,
with everybody as much as possible on one fair average—
sympathizes with those below the average,
but neglects those above the average, like Kees Mouw and Mrs. Hospers.
Orange City allows every individual to make the cash he can
any way he can,
sympathizes with those who turn out above average,
but neglects those below the average."

It seemed odd for him to mention
Marian Hospers and Kees Mouw
in the same breath
but otherwise it made sense.

Next morning the sick cow was out of the holes
lined up with the others
waiting to be milked.

After milking we went to Kees Mouw's shack
in Orange City
with five dollars.
He expected to be paid only if the animal got well
and always five dollars.

## 14. *Guest*

During spring break
of my sophomore year at college
my college choir visited Sioux County.
My parents and I had a college chum as a guest
for the weekend.

"These little towns are all the same," my chum said.
"How can you bear to spend a whole summer?"

I tried a defense:
"Take Sioux Center,
an open western town,
a major highway is its main street,
open to expansion in all directions,
egalitarian:
bring me your tired and your poor.
Orange City's main street is at right angles to the highway.
Main street and the highway are hidden from each other by the college.
Orange City doesn't want the whole world looking in
or moving down.
Main street is self-contained,
blocked by the college and a dwelling at either end;
main street will never be longer than just so long.
The number of people and businesses worthy
to occupy main street will always be a limited number.
The two most elegant buildings in the county,
Northwestern College's Zwemer Hall and the courthouse,
are both in Orange City.
Orange City is aristocratic."

And he:
"It was the same chocolate chip cookies and angel food cake
that the ladies served in Sioux Center and Orange City.
They could have carried it from one town to the other."

And I:
"The same recipe books in both towns, sure.
The ladies aid cookbooks borrow from each other."

And he:
"And when we had breakfast in the Central Cafe in Sioux Center,
the waitress said,
'If this nice weather keeps up
the farmers will be in the fields next week.'
Next day we had breakfast in Corner Cafe in Orange City,
and guess what the waitress said?"



And I:
"All right,
all waitresses here comment on the weather,
but you don't understand an area where farming is the only industry
and therefore is everybody's business,
including the restaurants'."

And he:
"You romanticize both towns
so that they are different from each other for you.
But there is no real difference."

And I:
"Listen,
why all the COOPs in Sioux Center?
Why Kees Mouw and Marian Hospers and BD Dykstra
all in Orange City?"

But he did not know Kees Mouw, Marian Hospers, or BD Dykstra.

In the land of the blind
the one-eyed man is sometimes not even able to carry off
being king.

## *15. The Last Word*

During the summer after my junior year at college
my parents' only enemy died in Hull.
I had understood the controversy only dimly,
but it involved joint investments,
religion,
and separate Christian schools—
all non-negotiables.
The trouble had been patched up,
but some of the hurt would need to wait
for a better world.

My parents would go to the funeral, they decided,
and I ought to go with them
to make it all look very much resolved.

Mother handled her anger in fierce understatement:
"I'll walk past the casket,
but I'm not going to look at him."
Exactly what she did.

I kept wondering how Dad would handle his anger.

A thundershower was in progress during the funeral.
Just as the casket was lifted into the hearse
lightning struck a maple across the street.
The rippling crash made the pallbearers stiffen.
Bark and twigs were still sifting down
when Dad said,
*"Ik geloof hij is aangekomen"*
("Seems to me he got there").

## *16. Dressing Up*

The June after graduating from college
with a music major
I played organ for a wedding in Orange City
and for another in Sioux Center.

Weddings had gone formal during my years away,
even to rented tuxedoes for the men,
even for the organist.

Everything was in order at the Orange City wedding.
The men wore tuxedoes as to the manner born.

Nobody had ordered my formal trousers for the Sioux Center wedding.
Only the part that shows needs dressing up.
I was in impeccable formal dress down to the waist
with blue overalls down below—
what I had worn to the church, expecting to change.
I was behind the fence at the organ
a half hour before any guest arrived.
Nobody noticed.
But in Sioux Center
we do not wear tuxedoes as to the manner born.

## *17. Evidence*

The following year I taught at Western Christian High in Hull
with a finger in music as well as in English.

One Friday evening in April
it was my duty to take the girls' trio
to a church in Sanborn to sing at a banquet
and then to a hayride party
at the home of one of the girls in Hospers.

After the banquet
the girls changed clothes for the hayride
and put their clothes in my car.

After the hayride
I delivered my remaining two passengers to their homes
in Orange City and Sioux Center.
They remembered some of their clothes,
but not all.

The next day my parents got me up early.
All of us were going to wash my car.
My mother found the circumstantial evidence:
a brassiere in my glove compartment.

Actually, she took it the way you would expect Sioux Center to.
She assumed my innocence and accepted my explanation.
She could even have accepted me guilty.
There was no girlfriend in sight for me then.
I was not married for another three years.
The brassiere had a reassuring effect on Mother.
There would probably be grandchildren from this son, too.

Dad took it the way you would expect Orange City to take it.
No number of cross-examinations revealed inconsistencies,
but neither did the cross-examinations put his mind at rest,
and so the cross-examinations continued.
When I was safely married three years later,
Dad must have been relieved
that the girls' trio
had not confronted me with a paternity suit.

## 18. *Basic Training*



The following year I went into the army.

The weather was rainy when I left home,
so the night before
we left the cars on the road at the end of the driveway
to be sure we could get out.

Mother and Aunty kissed me goodbye in the house,
dry-eyed.
This was happening in all kinds of families,
there might be a good reason to cry later,
but not now.
It was an egalitarian, Sioux Center goodbye.

Dad walked with me to the car at the end of the driveway,
hugged me,
and then, as I got into the car,
his legs went weak,
he fell in the middle of the road,
and sobbed.
Goodbyes were going on in all kinds of Sioux County homes
but this was his son and special.
It was an aristocratic, Orange City goodbye.

I rushed to pick him up,
but Klaas, my brother, said,
"Let him be, Sietze.
You can only make it worse.
He needs to be left alone.
I'll come back when I've brought you to the courthouse."
I was Sioux Center and Klaas Orange City.

We stopped at BD Dykstra's on the way.
He shook hands cordially,
but disowned me as a friend
because I had not declared myself a conscientious objector
in spite of our long talks on the subject.
The ceremoniousness was Orange City,
the pacifism a strange flowering of Sioux Center egalitarianism.

An Orange City pastor prayed with us recruits
and invited us to see him on furlough
or to write him about any problem at all.
The ceremoniousness was pure Orange City.



Then we were off to Sioux Falls by bus.
The Sioux Center boys had always been mild swearers and mild drinkers.
The Orange City boys were traditionally straight arrows,
abhorring sin.

The change was observable already on the way to Sioux Falls:
Sioux Center boys continued to swear mildly.
Orange City boys had suddenly acquired from somewhere
an amazing repertoire of oaths.

Throughout basic training I ran into Sioux County boys:
Sioux Center boys continued to drink mildly, usually one beer.
Orange City boys had suddenly mastered the terminology of mixed drinks.

Later the difference was evident in Japan.
Sioux Center boys flirted aggressively with Japanese office girls.
Orange City boys seemed to demand more than flirting.

In basic training, I was given a mess kit
that had been packed in cosmolene since World War I.
I could not wash it clean with soap or kerosene
or scour it clean with steel wool.
When hot food got into it,
it left a bad taste
and my stomach got upset from it.
I went on sick call.
When the doctor had heard my complaint, he asked:
"Soldier, do you like the army?"

"No sir,
but all I'm asking for is a clean mess kit."

"Soldier,
I'm sending you for psychological counseling."

So once a week I saw the psychiatrist,
and the two of us delved into my past,
my family relationships,
Orange City and Sioux Center.



One day on the rifle range
a large Black man and I were working together in the pits,
hauling down a target when the command was "Cease firing,"
patching it,
and shoving the patched one up
when the command was "Targets up,"
the targets riding against each other on pullies like wire stretchers.

"Targets up" the command came over the loudspeaker
and ours wouldn't budge.
Actually, it was because the Black man and I
were pulling against each other.
In desperation I leapt onto the target
just as the Black man gave a giant's heave,
and, my reflexes not being the best,
I rode up on the target.
For an instant I was in the line of fire.
"Cease firing! Cease firing!
Who was it climbed up on that target?"
I raised my hand.
"Oh, it's that psycho who sees the shrink every week."

The next week the psychiatrist knew what had happened on the range.
I tried to explain that it had been an accident.
For psychiatrists, as for God, there are no accidents.

That very week,
ten weeks into a sixteen-week cycle,
I was suddenly taken out of high-risk paratrooper training
and put into training to be a clerk-typist,
a low-tension position.

At the end of clerk-typist school,
getting ready to go home on furlough
and to be sent to Japan,
hundreds of soldiers and I
were getting overseas shots one day—
hundreds of naked soldiers walking in long lines.
My health form was thrust into my hands to carry,
and after my name I read my diagnosis:
"Schizoid personality, chronic and severe."

My Calvinism had taught me I was totally depraved,
and when my father routinely asked,
"What are all your good works and righteousness like?"
I would automatically answer, "Filthy rags,"
and he would smile at how well I knew my doctrine.

I was walking in the raw when I saw my diagnosis,
but the wind I shivered in blew straight off the Sea of Mortality,
and I knew that someone as basically flawed as I
could become useful only through a miracle of grace.

The resolution has come since—
accepting the unflattering truth
and letting God turn weakness into strength,
an imaginative memory being one of the symptoms of a schizoid personality.
The resolution has come,
continues to come,
and still will be coming,
for it does not yet appear what we shall be—
but I left for my furlough desolate.

I could not burden my parents with the diagnosis.
I could not talk to my own pastor in Middleburg—
suppose he broke confidentiality.

So I saw a Sioux Center pastor.
His advice turned out to be egalitarian.
He suggested I get a camera and take pictures in Japan.
It was the same advice he had given our neighborlady
suffering from postpartum depression.
It was the same advice he was to give his granddaughter
two decades later, then my student,
taking drugs and dropping out of school.
His one egalitarian remedy for all problems:
get a camera.



So I saw the Orange City pastor who had prayed so earnestly
when we left the courthouse,
inviting our confidences.
His advice turned out to be moralistic and aristocratic.
"Your schizoid personality," he said,
"comes from certain bad habits during your teens."
That was the moralistic part.
Then came the aristocratic part,
odd, but it let me know that I was special:
"Be glad it turned inside.
It seldom turns inward,
but that way it does not show.
When it stays outside,
it shows up disgusting:
hair on the palms."

Neither clergyman was much help
but each was in character for his town.

Leaving after my furlough was my farewell
to Sioux Center and Orange City.

I attribute my schizoid personality
to being the son of an Orange City father and a Sioux Center mother
and to being from Middleburg,
both and neither.

## *19. Epilogue*

And which town has the class,
Orange City or Sioux Center?
Depends on where you come from.

If you are from Orange City
and say Orange City has the class,
you have just turned whatever class Orange City has claim to
into style.
Why, you probably even believe
the Chamber of Commerce brochures
that come out at Tulip Festival.

If you are from Sioux Center
and say Orange City has only style,
you have no more than style in Sioux Center.
Sioux Center has its Chamber of Commerce brochures, too.
They read word-for-word like Orange City's,
in spite of the contrasts between the towns
by which you can tell that the brochures are false.

Consider Middleburg for class.
It has no Chamber of Commerce,
no store or gas station (both closed),
only one Reformed church now
(since the Christian Reformed church closed),
a thriving cemetery, its population quadrupling
the village population of thirty-nine.
Middleburg is not large enough for style—
a tiny pendant emerald weighing toward the north
on an imaginary chain,
one end fastened at Orange City,
the other at Sioux Center.

I will not say Middleburg has class,
lest all its class turn style,
but consider Middleburg for class.

O citizens of Orange City and Sioux Center, consider Middleburg,
which is to say,
O citizens of Sioux City and Sioux Falls, consider Doon,
which is to say,
O citizens of Minneapolis and Des Moines, consider Pipestone,
which is to say,
O citizens of New York and Chicago, consider Grand Rapids,
which is to say,
O citizens of Grand Rapids and Detroit, consider Rudyard,
which is to say,
O citizens of Tokyo and Yokohama, consider Nikko,
which is to say,
O citizens of The Hague and Amsterdam, consider Elspeth,
which is to say,
O citizens of Chichester and Brighton, consider Bognor Regis,

since considering yourselves citizens of the world automatically cancels that citizenship,
since the international style of the metropolis can only ever be style,
and since style without class is a sounding gong and tinkling cymbal.

## 20. *First Coda*

**song for person upon discovery of the lack of class in his/her quality of life: The Genevan Psalm 51, stanza 3 (7-10), to be sung in the manner of a plainsong:**

## 21. *Second Coda*

song for community upon discovery of the lack of class in its quality of life: The Genevan Psalm 51 stanza 6 (18-19), to be sung in parts:

Build - ing the cit - y's walls turns in - to joy
As liv - ing sa - cri - fice re - pla - ces du - ty.
May sin - ners turn to saints in your em - ploy,
Com - mun - i - ty re - veal a - new your beau - ty.

## 22. *Envoy*

Go, litel bok, go, litel myn homilie,
go to Sioux Center, Middleburg, Orange City,
and, since no foolishness goes on in them
but it goes on in anybody's town,
go, litel bok, to anybody's town,
laugh at innaccuracy, unfairness, wickedness,
stupidity and smugness, selfishness and greed.

Go, litel bok, flawed as you need to be,
done by a schizoid personality, chronic and severe—
go, litel bok, and say to all who read:
"My author's inaccurate, unfair, and wicked,
stupid, smug, selfish, greedy—lost."

Go, litel bok, your author shares his carrot.
He tugged at the orange-gold, grown all impacted
in crusty custom and official report.
When laughter fell to soften it, he tugged and tugged,
tugged just below the green top of the carrot,
until he cried to his laughter, "*Schei uit, schei uit*"
just as the carrot gave.

Should other carrots give, should readers fall
backwards, legs in the air, with laughter
crying out "*Schei uit!*" but resting softly
on their buoyancies, clutching orange-gold carrots:
then may your readers share their carrots, too.

Go, litel bok, go, litel pack of lies,
and be the truth.

# GLOSSARY

## A Rough-and-ready Middleburg Glossary

**Ames:** Home of Iowa State University, originally an agricultural school. Its aims are sometimes self-contradictory—promoting the invention of poisons and campaigning against their use—and usually at odds with the aims of Middleburg.

**Arminians:** Followers of Jacobus Arminius (Jacob Harmensen, 1560-1609), whose views on the freedom of the human will did not find favor with the Synod of Dordt (1618-1619). Recent scholarship has shown that even his enemies considered Arminius a Calvinist. Middleburg, however, distinguished rigorously between Calvinists and Arminians, the latter also called "Fundamentalists."

**Beatrix, Queen:** Monarch of the Netherlands from 1981 until the present. Sister in all Middleburg families.

**bloat:** Common digestive ailment of cows that eat too many fresh green corn plants. Fatal, if the cow is not stopped from eating her fill.

**Bognor Regis:** A resort town on the southern coast of England, called *Bognor* until George V went there to recuperate from tuberculosis. Upon his recovery, the city fathers asked the king whether he would give permission to add the *Regis,* "of the king." "Call it whatever you like," the king is reported to have said, "as long as I do not need to ever go there again." Bognor Regis and Middleburg, Iowa, share the same spirit, for which reason the reported statement of George V strikes people who know both places as not very classy. It would never have occurred to a member of the House of Orange (or any other kingly house) to have said such a thing.

**budget:** A quasi-tax levied by Reformed churches. The total projected annual expense of the church is divided by the number of families of the church. The tax strikes some members of the RCAM and CRCM as curiously at variance with the principle of Christian liberty and with Paul's declaration that "the Lord loves a cheerful giver," but liberty and cheerfulness never get enough money to support the church, as the RCAM and the CRCM, alas, have learned from sad experience.

**catechism:** Passing on the funded wisdom of the church by having children learn prescribed answers to prescribed questions. Sunday school was barely tolerated in the CRCM, as a foreign import from Methodism; Sunday school was held only during the summer, when catechism lessons were not held. Sunday school has always been the more thriving of the two institutions at the RCAM.



**censura morum:** A ceremony conducted in consistories four times a year, during the week preceding Communion. Each elder and deacon is asked whether he has any reason for displeasure with any of his colleagues in their carrying out of the duties of their offices.

**check:** Planting corn in equidistant rows like a checkerboard, so that even the diagonals are clear. Bad for erosion, but very tidy.

**Christian Reformed Church:** The Reformed Church in America (RCA) is parallel to the state church in the Netherlands. The CRC is parallel to the *Gereformeerdekerken* in the Netherlands, dissenting groups against their respective parent bodies. All this is complicated by the fact that the RCA churches in Sioux County were first called *Gereformeerd*—their establishment itself in the new land being construed as dissent against the Dutch state church.

**Christiansen, F. Melius:** Founder and director of the St. Olaf College Choir, the first group in America to renew and popularize the ancient art of singing without accompaniment. Brought the Lutheran chorales into prominence in the American musical world. Would he had turned a Calvinist and done the same for The Genevan Psalter.

**classis:** The ruling body of churches in one Reformed denomination and in one geographical area. The CRCM was in Classis Orange City. Classis meets in the spring and in the fall.

**collection plate:** Large wooden plates which are passed through the congregation to gather the tithes, offerings, and budget envelopes of the faithful, the three being not mutually exclusive.

**Communion:** "The Lord's Supper," eating bread and drinking wine (in the CRCM) or grape juice (in the RCAM) in memory of Christ's death and with an awareness of his presence.

**Confession of Faith:** To Reformed Christians what Confirmation is to the Catholics, Anglicans, and Lutherans. It consists of an oral examination on faith and doctrine by the consistory, a public ceremony of answering affirmatively to several prescribed questions, and first communion. The average age is between 16 and 20, somewhat older than in non-Reformed denominations.

**consistory:** The ruling body of a local Reformed church. The RCAM and the CRCM had separate consistories. This word is defined here for readers from Alton and other Roman Catholic communities, for whom a consistory is an assembly of all the cardinals in the Vatican, presided over by the pope.

**consistory room:** Not the Sistine Chapel, as readers from Alton will think, but an annex to the sanctuary in which the consistory meets before the service to have prayer with the pastor; from the consistory room the pastor leads an ecclesiastical procession of elders and deacons into the sanctuary—the sight of whom inspires as much awe in the young as a consistory of cardinals would, because the young would not even know what a cardinal is. The procession is more impressive in the RCAM than in the CRCM, because in CRCM it takes place during the organ prelude, but in the RCAM it takes place after the prelude and before the opening hymn, in stark silence.

**cosmolene:** Heavy grease. A word not native to Middleburg. Introduced by servicemen on furlough.

**covenant of grace:** The Reformed doctrine that God's promise to Abraham—to be his God and the God of his children—is renewed with every new child born to Christian parents. The Reformed basis for the baptizing of infants.

**CRC:** The Christian Reformed Church.

**CRCM:** The Christian Reformed Church of Middleburg, defunct since 1959.

**dominie:** As Catholics call their priests "Father," so Reformed Christians in Middleburg call their pastors "dominie," from Latin, *dominus*, meaning "Lord."

**Doon:** A small town on the Rock River in Northwest Iowa known for its colorful history and for its weekly newspaper, the *Doon Press*, where any kind of news can appear next to any other kind of news. By thus resisting the current journalistic style of departmentalization, the *Press* preserves its readers from the fragmentation of life presented by most other media.

**Dordt:** The Synod which decided against the Arminians in 1618-1619 in the city of Dordt. Also a liberal-arts college in Sioux Center, Iowa, named after the great Synod.

**excommunication:** Depriving members of a church of the right of partaking of Communion or of having their children baptized, on the grounds of unconfessed sin or doctrinal error.

**Frisian:** A Germanic language, distinct from both English and Dutch although sharing characteristics of both. It has had an unbroken literary tradition for a longer time than have Dutch or English. Its speakers, in the North of the Netherlands, are thought by the speakers of the other Dutch dialects to be stubborn and depressed. The Frisians murdered St. Boniface, not for his faith, the legend goes, but because the English missionary referred to Frisian as a speech impediment. A great oak in Dokkum is pointed out to tourists as the spot where the murder took place in 755.

**The Genevan Psalter:** John Calvin's Psalter of 1562, which in turn is the basis for Dutch Psalter of 1773, which preserves all the same melodies in the same order. It is Calvinism's only liturgical treasure. The most familiar of the Genevan melodies is the common Protestant Doxology: "Praise God from Whom All Blessings Flow." A less familiar melody is Psalm 51, the Calvinist *kyrie.* The Scottish Psalter, while using many Genevan melodies, assigns them to different psalms from the original. "Praise God," the doxology mentioned above, is "Old Hundredth" in the Scottish Psalter, but the tune for Psalm 134 in the Genevan Psalter. The Genevan Psalm 100 has a melody totally different from "Old Hundredth." The *Psalter Hymnal* follows the original Genevan Psalter in its melody for Psalms 100 and 134.



**The Hague:** Seat of the government of the Netherlands.

**The Heidelberg Catechism:** A Reformed Catechism from the year 1534. Its outline is the basis for the folk theology carried out in all Reformed communities: I. Sin and Misery, II. Deliverance, and III. Gratitude. Its first question precedes the outline, and is an index to the tone of the whole document: "What is your only comfort in life and in death?" The document is the basis for the oral examination which is the major component of Confession of Faith. One of two sermons each Sunday is required to be preached on a portion of this document, according to the canon law of the CRC. The love-hate attitude of Reformed Christians toward this document is particularly intense, since it is a symbol at once of their liberation and of their bondage.

**Het Spul Draait:** *"The Whole Works Turns,"* the title of a Frisian play about Galileo by B.D. Dykstra.

**Hoeksema, Herman:** Founder of the Protestant Reformed denomination, which severed itself from the Christian Reformed Church over the issue of God's love for the non-elect, Hoeksema taking the severe view; in 1924. Middleburg has never had a church of this persuasion, but Hull, Orange City, Sioux Center, and Doon do or did have. Families left the CRCM to attend preferred services in Hull. The festering scars of the break have still not healed.

**hog ring:** An open metal ring, pierced shut with a special pliers into the nose of a hog to prevent its rooting in the mud.

**homily:** What Middleburg connoisseurs of sermons call a sermon that does not make it.

**The House of Orange:** The royal family of the Netherlands; what the Windsors are to England.

**huisbezoek:** A yearly visit by the dominie and an elder to every Reformed family in order to appraise spiritual progress on the part of every family member. The questioner, usually the dominie, addresses himself in turn to every member of the family, from oldest to youngest. Testimonies are restricted to this time, unlike the testimonies of fundamentalists, which have no prescribed time or place but go on at any time, without preparation, and most often inappropriately.



**Juliana, Queen:** Reigned over the Netherlands from 1948 until 1980. Aunty in all Middleburg families.

**Kuyper, Abraham:** Founder of the Free University of Amsterdam in 1880. Prime Minister of the Netherlands from 1901 until 1905; Queen Wilhelmina's first Prime Minister. Developed the theory of "sphere sovereignty," that God is to be acknowledged as sovereign not only in the Church, but in every sphere of human activity. Implicit in this theory is the distinction between Christ's Church and Christ's Kingdom: the Church preaches the gospel and administers the sacraments, but the Kingdom brings society progressively under the sovereignty of God. Preoccupied with the need for social change, Kuyper stressed the parent-controlled Christian school as the best instrument for effecting such change. The CRC has followed Kuyper's policy in establishing such parent-controlled schools, free from state control, though CRC parents have not always remembered Kuyper's rationale for establishing such schools: social change. The CRC is regarded as more Kuyperian than the RCA; yet when Kuyper visited Orange City in 1898, he was the house guest of Henry Hospers, churchman in the RCA, and Kuyper appeared in more audiences of the RCA than of the CRC—which makes one wonder whether the polarization between RCA and CRC over Kuyper and Christian schools is not of recent date, and trivial.

**Kuyperians:** Followers of Abraham Kuyper. A rule of thumb for telling Kuyperians from non-Kuyperians, learned from Mattheis Roubos, member of the RCAM in full communion, but member of the CRCM "Men's Society": "When your relatives become ministers or missionaries and you are a Kuyperian, you never say that these relatives have gone into 'full-time Kingdom work,' since every Kuyperian—whether a stockyards manager, a seed-corn salesman, or a school teacher—considers himself to be in full-time Kingdom work." "Full-time Kingdom work" was for Theis Roubos a meaningless redundancy. Non-Kuyperian members of all Reformed denominations borrowed the term "full-time Kingdom work" from American Fundamentalism. The way Fundamentalists use the term, it covers the missionary but not the seed-corn salesman, whose duty for God is complete only if he makes more and more money so that he can help support more and more missionaries.

Another rule-of-thumb for telling Kuyperians from non-Kuyperians: Kuyperians prefer the Genevan Psalm tunes; non-Kuyperians prefer the contemporary hymns of Bill Gaither. This test is my own intuitive one, but none the less reliable for that.

**op gereformeerde grondslag:** "Done on the Reformed basis," that is, on the theory of sphere sovereignty.



**Psalter Hymnal:** The song book prescribed for church services in the CRC. More and more Genevan psalms are being included in each edition, particularly under the influence of church musicians, who are interested in liberating themselves from the shackles of the nineteenth-century hymn.

**RCA:** The Reformed Church in America.

**RCAM:** The Reformed Church of Middleburg, also called the Free Grace Church.

**Reformed:** Reformational. Pertaining to the Reformed Church in America, the Christian Reformed Church, the Protestant Reformed Church, the Netherlands Reformed Church, or any other Calvinistic denomination.

**Rockford socks:** Brown and white woolen socks worn by men for farm work and never to church. Never worn to town, unless a part broke on the machine and you had to rush to town to buy a spare part; then you still changed your socks to go to Orange City but not to go to Sioux Center.

**Sandy Hollow:** Called "the sandpit" formerly, it was our swimming hole. Now that a bath house and lifeguards are provided, it has been given a rustic name.

**schei uit:** "Quit it," "Cut it out!"

**tiddlywinks:** Game in which one snaps discs the size of a quarter into a low container the size of a cup. Played in Middleburg only during blizzards.

**weed commissioner:** A farmer hired by the county to inspect every farm for "noxious weeds," as the document read. (Everybody always used to call them *notious* weeds, even the weed commissioner.) He was a nice man and came in for coffee, but an agent of Ames, who wanted nothing more than to strew mysterious poisons on your field to justify his salary. So when, after coffee, he asked, "Do you people have any notious weeds?" you always answered, "No." That afternoon you would make your own mixture of kerosene, crankcase oil, and salt, pull the Russian thistles, and spray the mixture to mark the spot. Russian thistles never came up in that spot the next year, but neither did anything else.

**Wilhelmina, Queen:** Reigned over the Netherlands from 1880 until 1948. Grandmother in all Middleburg families.

**Zoestdijk:** Palace home of Queen Juliana near Utrecht.